JOHN MAYER ANTHOLOGY FOR EASY GUITAR
VOLUME 1

CONTENTS

This book was approved by John Mayer

Arranged by Jeff Jacobson and Steve Gorenberg

Cherry Lane Music Company
Director of Publications/Project Editor: Mark Phillips
Project Coordinator: Rebecca Skidmore

ISBN 978-1-60378-247-0

Visit our website at www.cherrylaneprint.com

BACK TO YOU

Words and Music by
John Mayer

I tried to for-get you, I tried to stay a-way, but it's too late. O-ver you, I'm nev-er o-ver, o-ver you. There's some-thing a-bout you, it's just the way you move, the way you move me.

Chorus

Yeah, I'm so good at for-get-ting,

E5   Aadd9/C♯   D⁶₉

and I ___ quit ___ ev - er - y game ___ I ___ play,

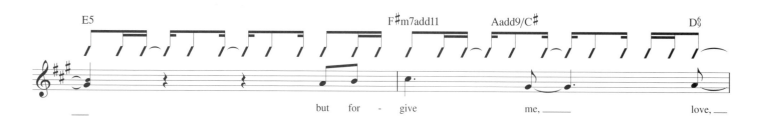

E5   F♯m7add11   Aadd9/C♯   D⁶₉

___ but for - give   me, _____   love, ___

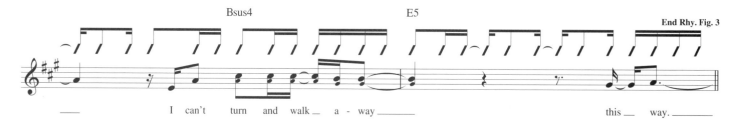

Bsus4   E5   **End Rhy. Fig. 3**

___ I can't turn and walk ___ a - way _____ this ___ way. _____

Interlude

Gtr. 1: w/ Rhy. Fig. 1

Asus2   F♯m11   Bm7add11   Eadd9   F♯m11

Verse

Gtr. 1: w/ Rhy. Fig. 2

A

2. Back ___ to you. It al - ways comes ___ a - round. ___

F♯m7

Back ___ to you. I walk with your ___ shad -

Bm7   Eadd9

- ow, ___ I'm sleep - ing in ___ my bed _____ with your ___

Chorus

Gtr. 1: w/ Rhy. Fig. 3

F♯7sus2   F♯m7   E5

___ sil - hou - ette. ___ Yeah, should have

BIGGER THAN MY BODY

Words and Music by
John Mayer

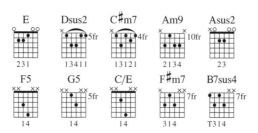

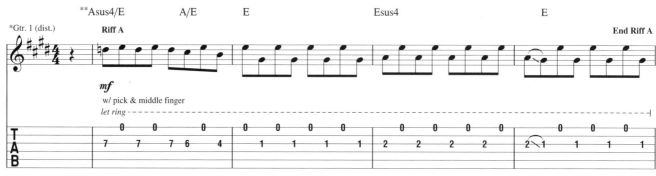

*Processed w/ Roger Linn Adrenalinn Pedal. The notes indicated are John Mayer's
actual parts; pedal generates random notes.

**Chord symbols reflect overall harmony.

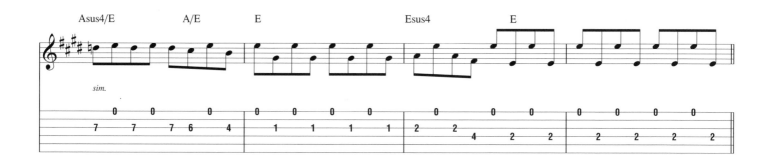

Verse

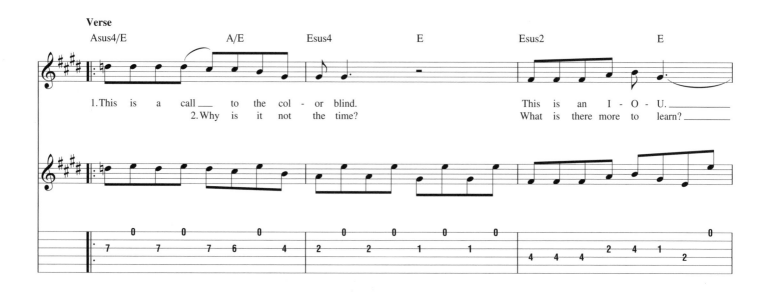

1. This is a call ___ to the col - or blind.
2. Why is it not the time?

This is an I - O - U. _____
What is there more to learn? _____

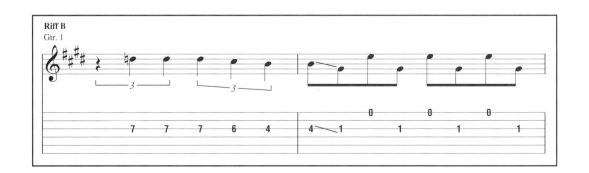

Interlude

Gtr. 1: w/ Rhy. Fig. 1 (2 times)

Bridge

Gtr. 2 tacet

Gtr. 1: w/ Rhy. Fig. 2 (4 times)

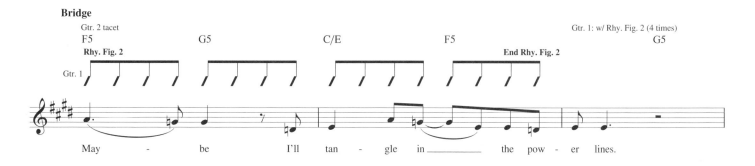

May - be I'll tan - gle in ____ the pow - er lines.

And it ___ might _____ be o - ver in _____ a sec - ond's time.

But I'll glad - ly _____ go down in a flame ___ if a flame's _

D.S. al Coda

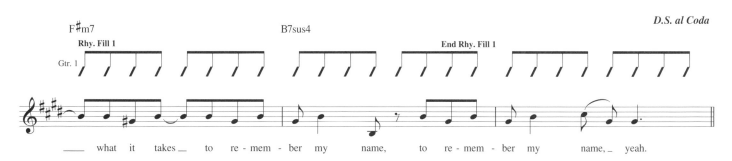

____ what it takes ___ to re - mem - ber my name, to re - mem - ber my name, _ yeah.

⊕ Coda

big- ger ____ than my bod - y. ____ I'm big- ger than my bod-

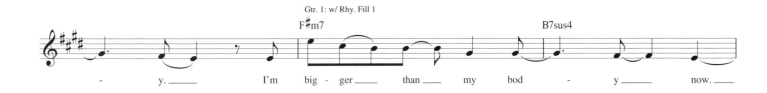

- y. ____ I'm big- ger ____ than ____ my bod - y ____ now. ____

Outro

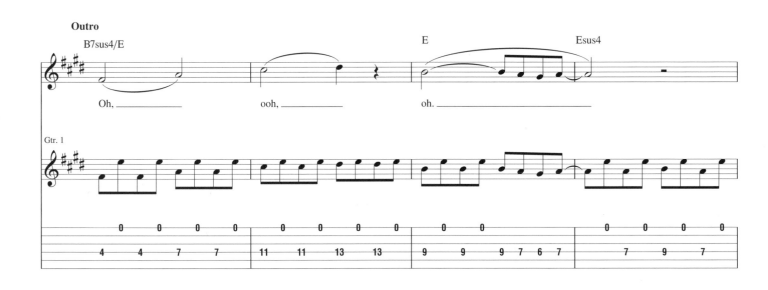

Oh, _____ ooh, _____ oh.

Gtr. 1

Begin fade   *Fade out*

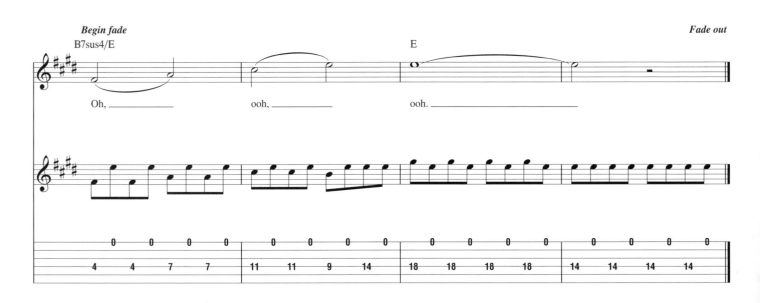

Oh, _____ ooh, _____ ooh. _____

CLARITY

Words and Music by
John Mayer

14

Interlude

Bridge

So much wast - ed in _____ the af - ter - noon. _____

So much sa - cred in _____ the month _

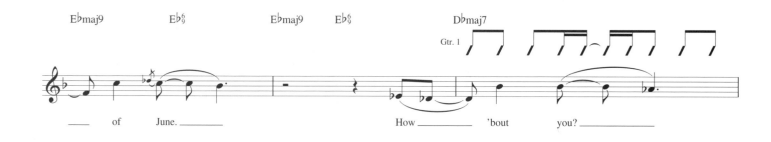

_____ of June. _____ How _____ 'bout you? _____

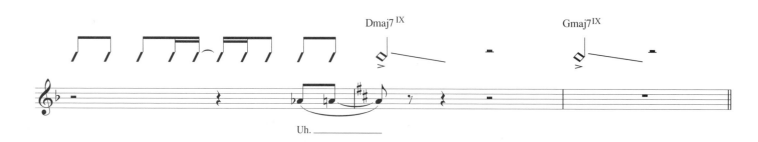

Uh. _____

Outro-Chorus

Gtr. 1: w/ Rhy. Fig. 3 (till end)

And I _____ will wait _____ to find _____

G   F#m   Bm

if this ___ will last ___ for - ev - er. ___ And I ___ will wait ___ to find ___

G   F#m   Bm   G   F#m   Bm

that it won't and it won't, and it won't. _____

G   F#m   Bm

And I ___ won't pay ___ no ___ mind _____ wor - ried 'bout ___ no rain - y weath - er. ___

G   F#m   Bm   G   F#m   Bm

And I ___ will waste ___ no ___ time _____ re - main -

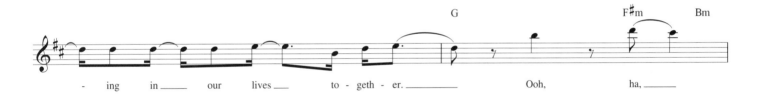

G   F#m   Bm

- ing in ___ our lives ___ to - geth - er. _____ Ooh, ha, _____

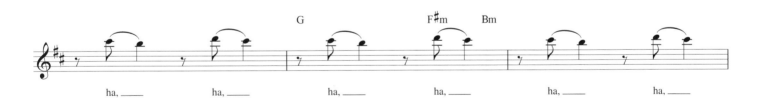

G   F#m   Bm

ha, ___ ha, ___ ha, ___ ha, ___ ha, ___ ha, ___

G   F#m   Bm   G   F#m   Bm

ha, ___ ha, _____ ooh. Ooh, _____ ooh, _____

Begin fade   *Fade out*

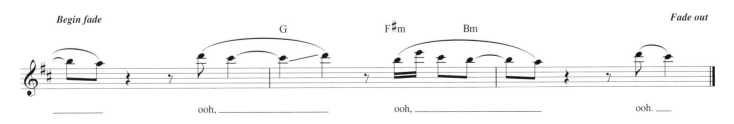

G   F#m   Bm

_____ ooh, _____ ooh, _____ ooh. ___

COME BACK TO BED

Words and Music by
John Mayer

sheets   and your foot - steps   are   down the hall.

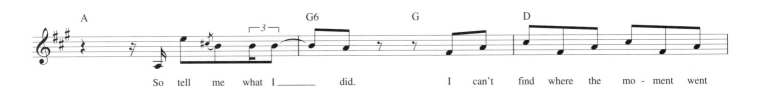

So   tell   me   what   I_____   did.   I   can't   find   where   the   mo - ment   went

𝄉 Pre-Chorus

wrong   at   all.   You _ can   be   mad   in   the   morn - ing.

I'll   take   back   what   I   said.   Just   don't   leave _

Chorus

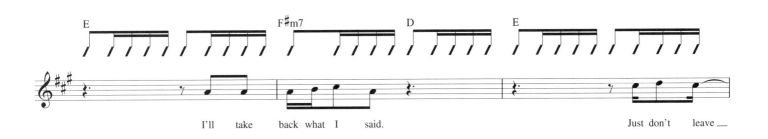

_ me   a - lone   here. _   It's   cold, ba - by.   Come   back   to   bed,

1st time, Gtr. 1: w/ Rhy. Fig. 2 (2 1/2 times)
2nd time, Gtr. 1: w/ Rhy. Fig. 2 (3 times)

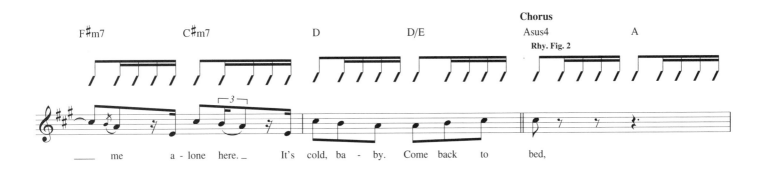

come   back   to   bed,   come   back   to   bed,

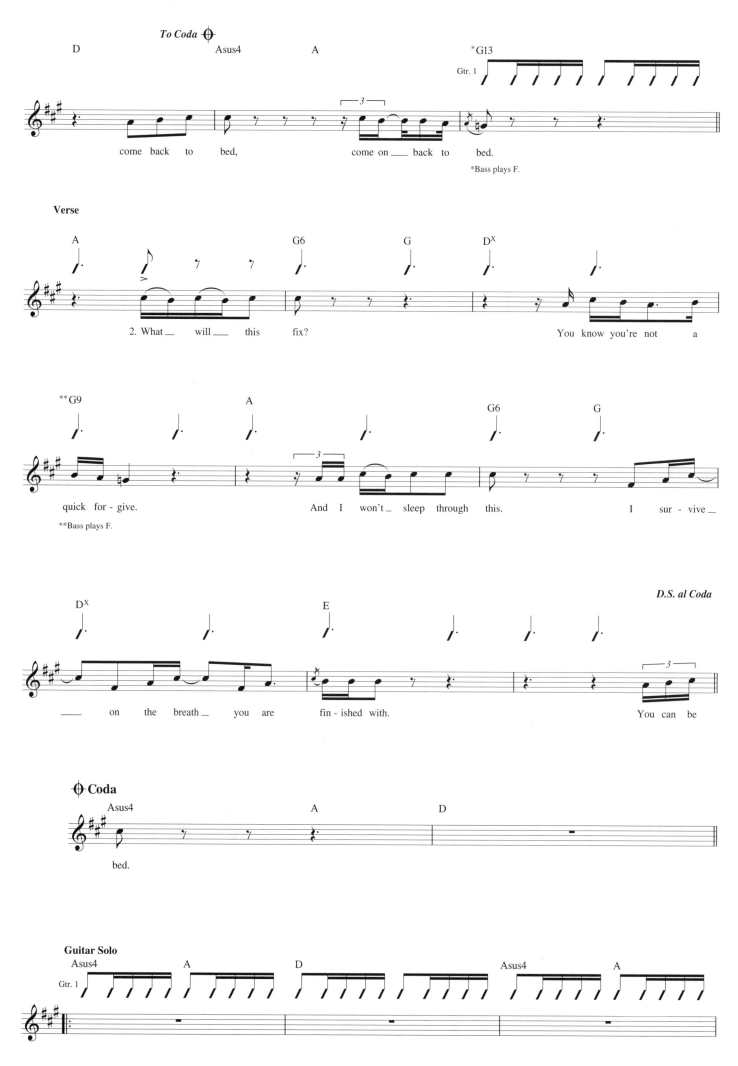

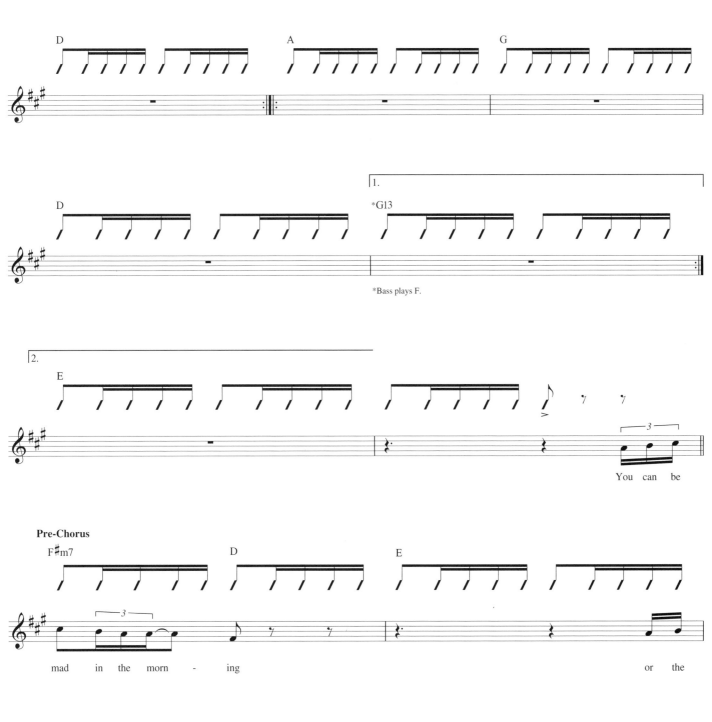

*Bass plays F.

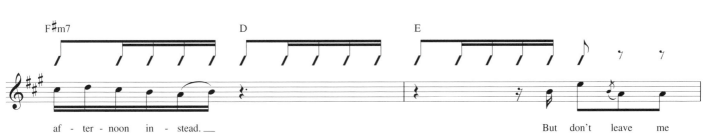

You can be

Pre-Chorus

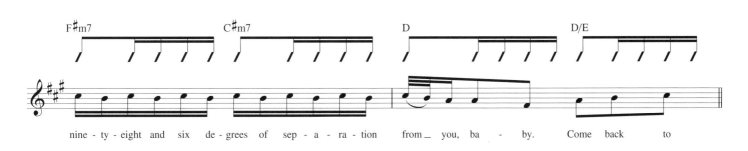

mad in the morn - ing or the

af - ter - noon in - stead. But don't leave me

nine - ty - eight and six de - grees of sep - a - ra - tion from you, ba - by. Come back to

Chorus

Gtr. 1 w/ Rhy. Fig. 2 (4 times)

bed, come back to bed,

come back to bed. Why don't you come ___ back to

Outro

Gtr. 1 w/ Rhy. Fig. 2 (4 times)

bed? Don't hold your love o - ver my

head. ___ Don't hold your love o - ver my

head. ___ Don't hold your love o - ver my

head. ___ Don't hold your love o - ver my

Gtr. 1

head. ___ Don't hold your love o - ver my

head. ___ Don't hold your love...

COMFORTABLE

Words and Music by
John Mayer and Clay Cook

Capo III

Intro

Moderately slow, in 2 ♩. = 56

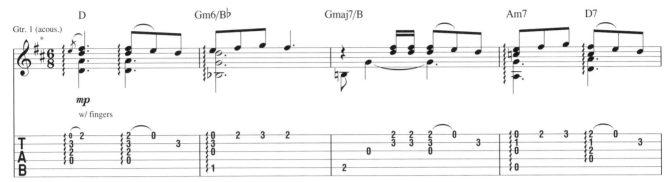

*All music sounds a minor 3rd higher than indicated due to capo. Capoed fret is "0" in tab.

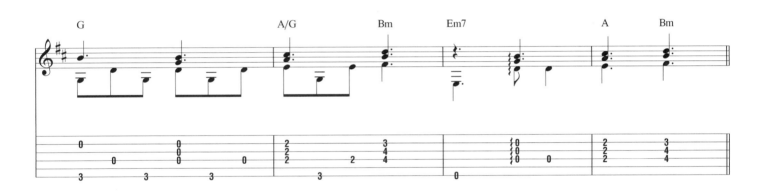

Verse

1. I just re-mem-bered that time at the mar-ket; snuck up be-hind ___ me and

sleep with this new ___ girl I'm still get-ting used ___ to. My friends all ap-prove, ___ say, "She's

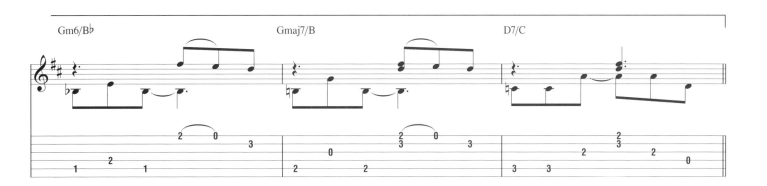

Pre-Chorus

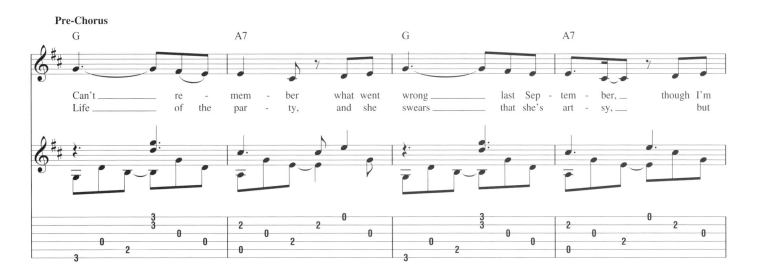

Can't _____ re - mem - ber what went wrong _____ last Sep - tem - ber, __ though I'm
Life _____ of the par - ty, and she swears _____ that she's art - sy, __ but

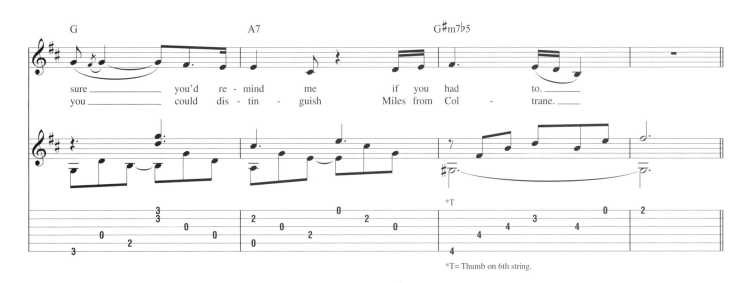

sure _____ you'd re - mind me if you had to. _____
you _____ could dis - tin - guish Miles from Col - trane. _____

*T

*T= Thumb on 6th string.

𝄋 Chorus

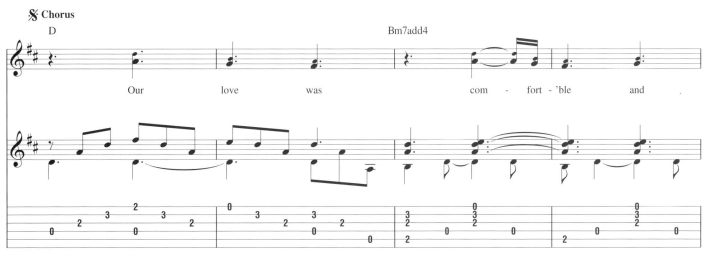

Our love was com - fort - 'ble and

*Downstemmed notes are strings arr. for gtr. (next 2 meas.).

Verse

3. She thinks I can't see the smile that she's fak-in' and pos-es for pic-tures that aren't being tak-en. I loved you; gray

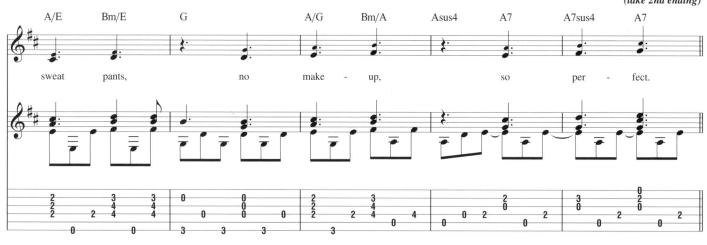

sweat pants,   no make - up,   so per - fect.

Coda

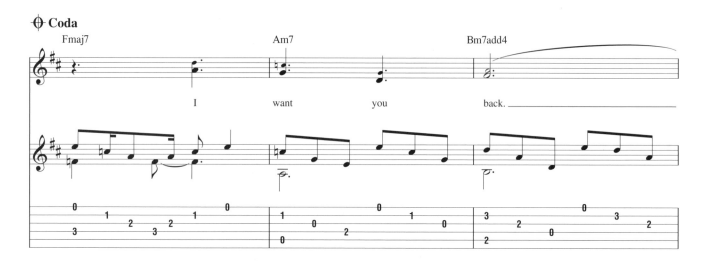

I want you back. ___

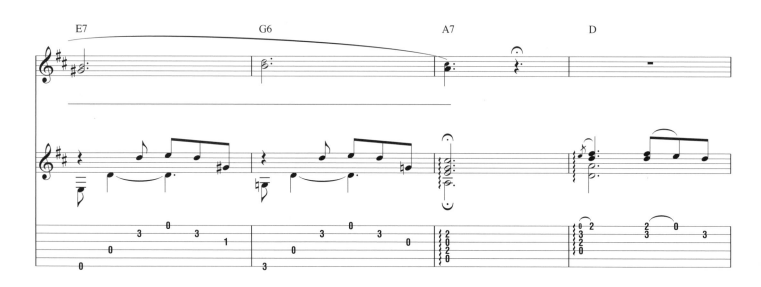

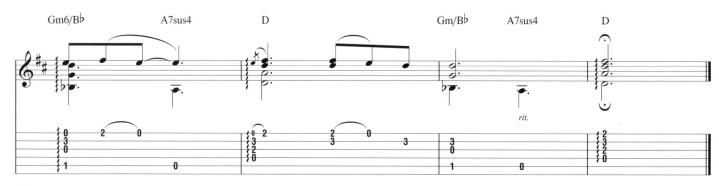

rit.

28

DAUGHTERS

Words and Music by
John Mayer

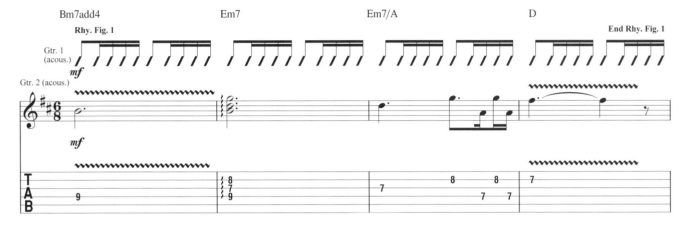

Intro
Slowly, in 2 ♩. = 44

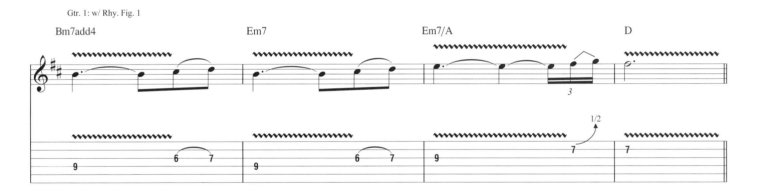

Gtr. 1: w/ Rhy. Fig. 1

Verse
Gtr. 1: w/ Rhy. Fig. 1 (4 times)
Gtr. 2 tacet

1. I _____ know a girl; _____ she puts the col - or in - side of my world. _____

_____ But she's just like a maze _____ where all of the walls _____

all continually change. And I've done all I
can to stand on her steps with my heart in my hand.
Now I'm starting to see maybe it's got nothing to do with me.

𝄋 Chorus

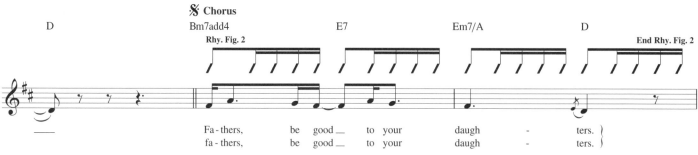

Fathers, be good to your daughters.
fathers, be good to your daughters.

Gtr. 1: w/ Rhy. Fig. 2 (3 times)

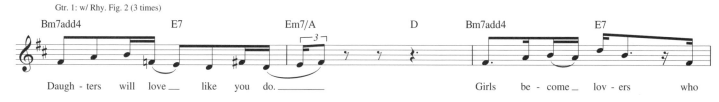

Daughters will love like you do. Girls become lovers who

To Coda 1 ⊕
To Coda 2 ⊕

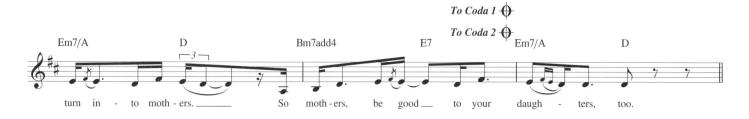

turn into mothers. So mothers, be good to your daughters, too.

Interlude

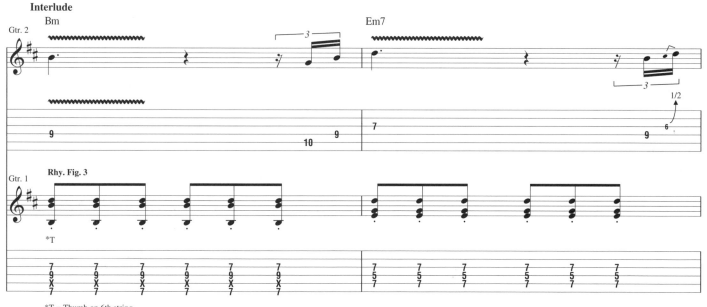

*T = Thumb on 6th string.

30

DREAMING WITH A BROKEN HEART

Words and Music by
John Mayer

*Piano arr. for gtr.

**Chord symbols reflect implied harmony.

1. When you're dream - ing with a bro - ken heart,

the wak - ing up is the hard - est part.

You roll out of bed and down on your knees,

and for a mo - ment you can hard - ly breathe. Won - der - ing

was she real - ly here? Is she

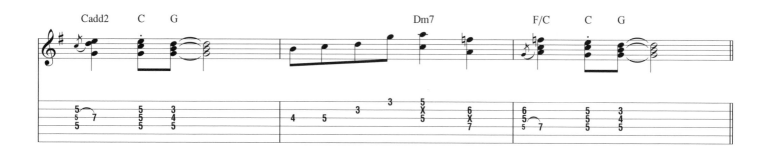

Interlude

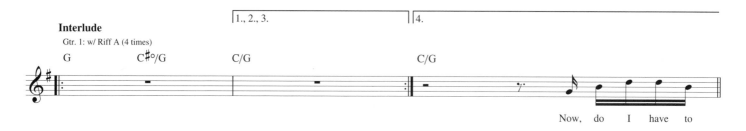

Now, do I have to

Bridge

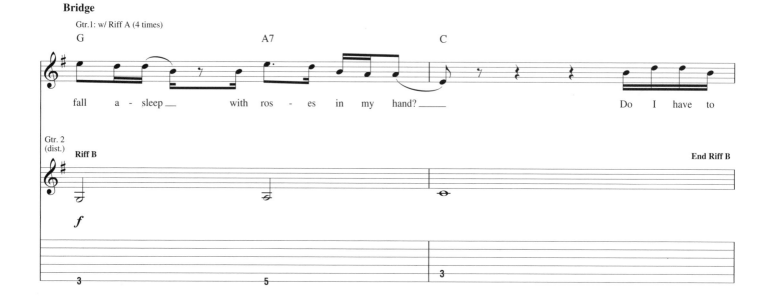

fall a - sleep ___ with ros - es in my hand? ___ Do I have to

fall a - sleep ___ with ros - es in my hand? ___ Now, do I have to

fall a - sleep ___ with ros - es in my hand? ___ Do I have to

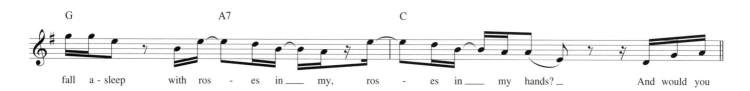

fall a - sleep with ros - es in ___ my, ros - es in ___ my hands? ___ And would you

FRIENDS, LOVERS OR NOTHING

Words and Music by
John Mayer

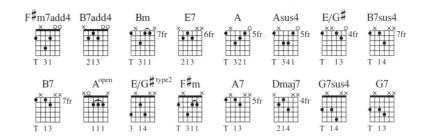

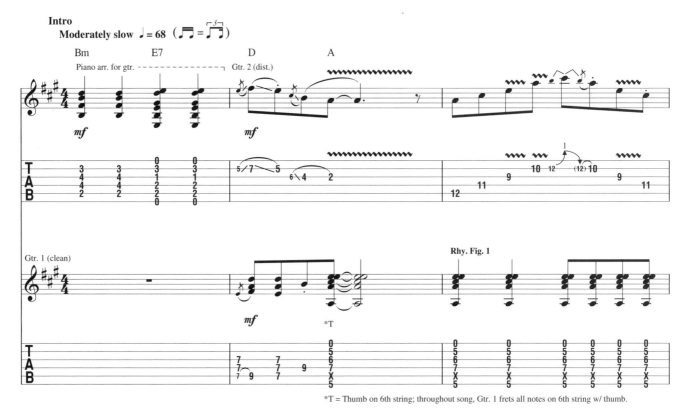

*T = Thumb on 6th string; throughout song, Gtr. 1 frets all notes on 6th string w/ thumb.

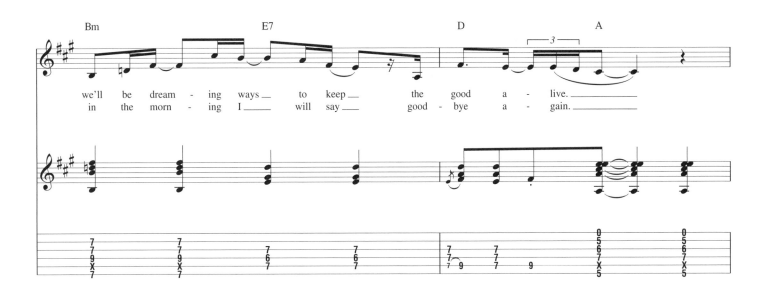

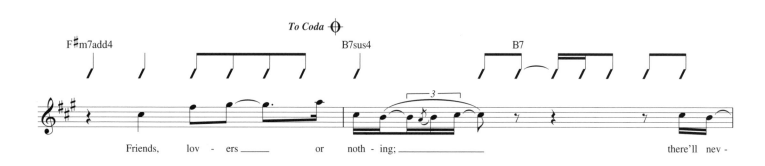

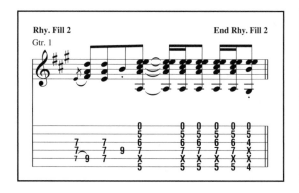

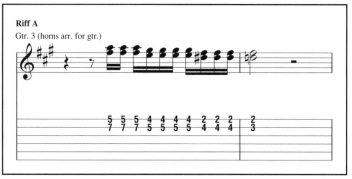

41

GRAVITY

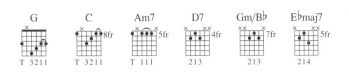

Words and Music by
John Mayer

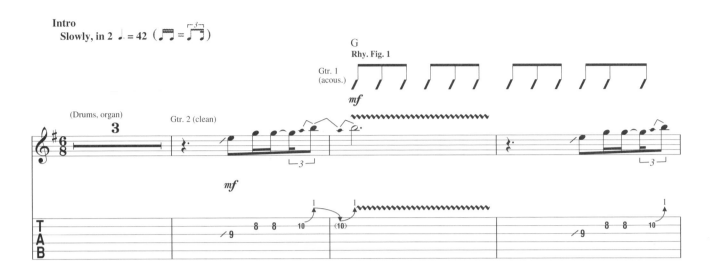

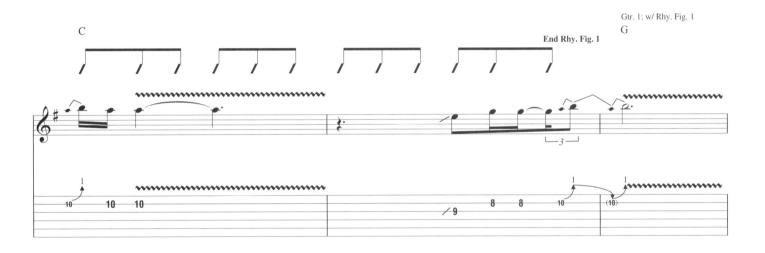

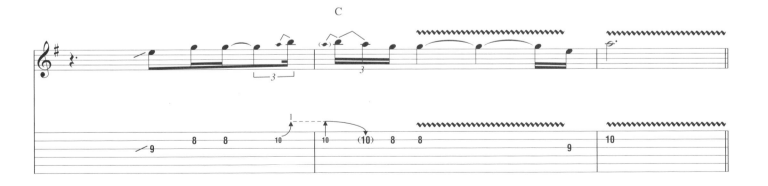

45

HALF OF MY HEART

Words and Music by
John Mayer

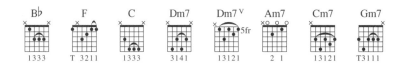

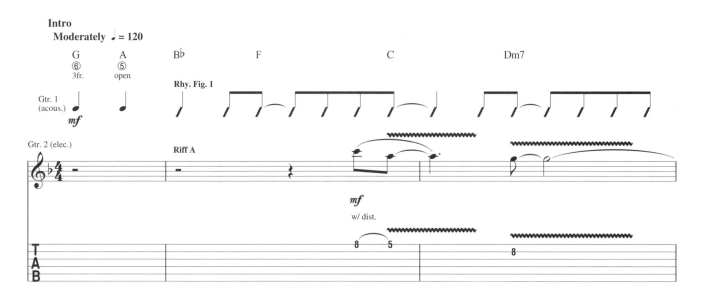

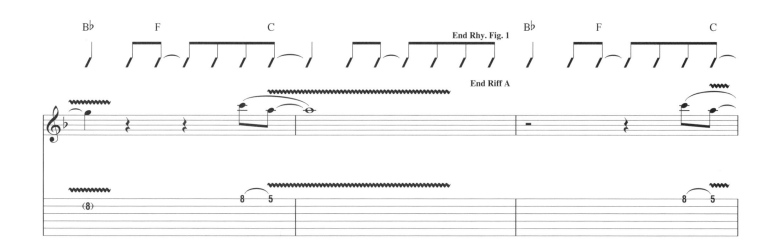

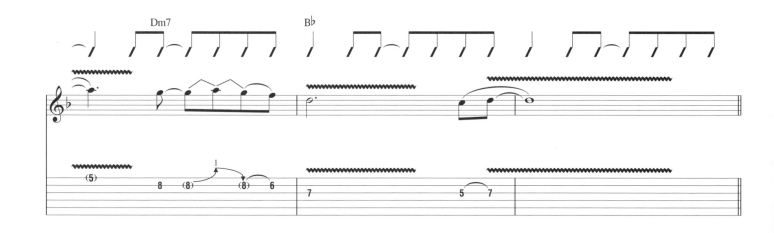

Chorus

half of my heart's _ got a grip on the sit-u-a-tion, half of my heart takes _ time. _

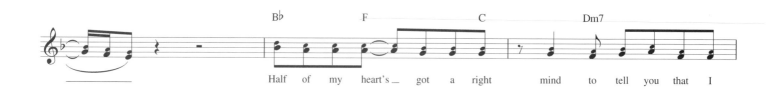

_ Half of my heart's _ got a right mind to tell you that I

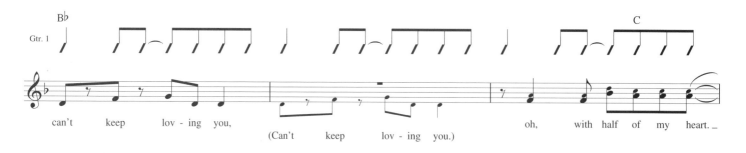

can't keep lov-ing you, (Can't keep lov-ing you.) oh, with half of my heart. _

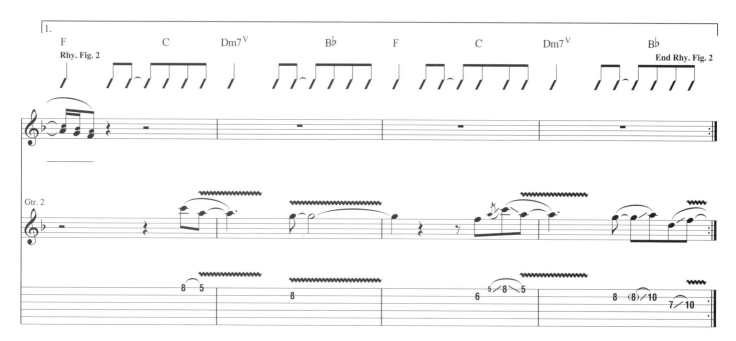

With half of my heart. _____ Your faith _

48

Bridge

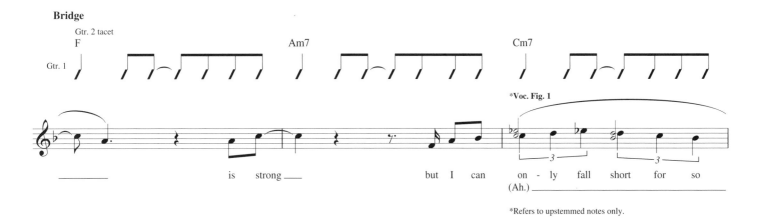

Gtr. 2 tacet
F · · · · Am7 · · · · Cm7 · · · ·

Gtr. 1

*Voc. Fig. 1

is strong ___ but I can on - ly fall short for so
(Ah.) _____

*Refers to upstemmed notes only.

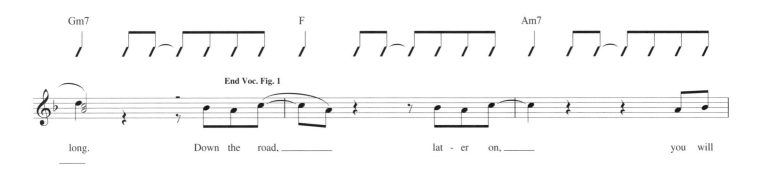

Gm7 · · · · F · · · · Am7 · · · ·

End Voc. Fig. 1

long. Down the road, ___ lat - er on, ___ you will

Bkgd. Voc.: w/ Voc. Fig. 1
Cm7 · · · · Gm7 · · · · B♭ · · · ·

hate that I nev - er gave more to you ___ than ___ half of my heart, ___

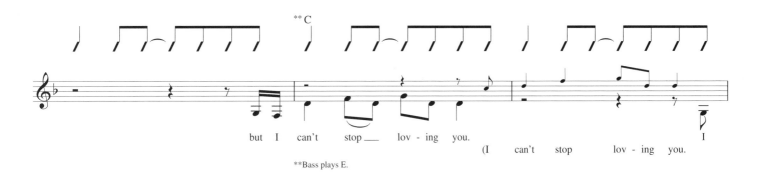

**C · · · ·

but I can't stop ___ lov - ing you. (I can't stop lov - ing you. I

**Bass plays E.

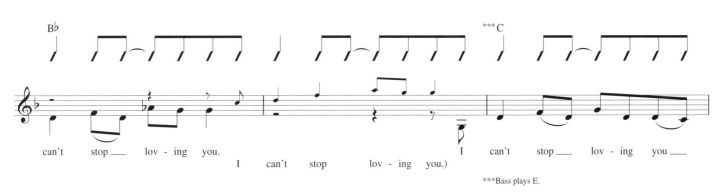

B♭ · · · · ***C · · · ·

can't stop ___ lov - ing you. I can't stop lov - ing you.) I can't stop ___ lov - ing you ___

***Bass plays E.

Interlude

Gtr. 1: w/ Rhy. Fig. 1
Gtr. 2: w/ Riff A

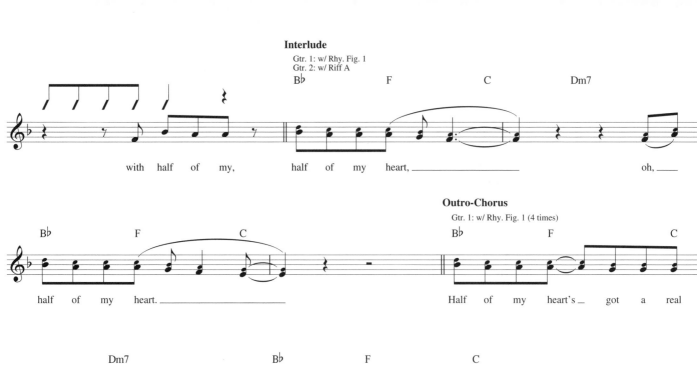

with half of my, half of my heart, _____ oh, ____

Outro-Chorus

Gtr. 1: w/ Rhy. Fig. 1 (4 times)

half of my heart. _____ Half of my heart's __ got a real

good i - mag - i - na - tion, half of my heart's __ got you. _____

Half of my heart's __ got a right mind to tell you that half of my heart __ won't do. __

Half of my heart __ is a shot - gun __ wed - ding to a bride __

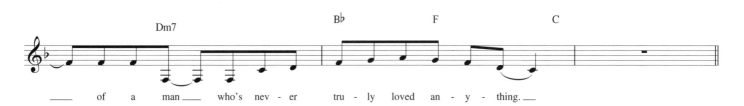

__ with a pa - per ring. __ And half of my heart __ is the part __

__ of a man __ who's nev - er tru - ly loved an - y - thing. __

Repeat and fade

w/ Bkgd. Voc. ad lib
Gtr. 1: w/ Rhy. Fig. 1

Half of my heart, ____ oh, __ half of my heart. _____

THE HEART OF LIFE

Words and Music by
John Mayer

Tune down 1/2 step:
(low to high) Eb-Ab-Db-Gb-Bb-Eb

Intro
Moderately, in 2 ♩ = 96

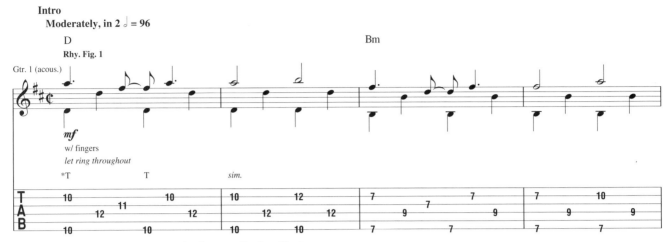

*T = L.H. thumb; throughout song fret all notes on 6th string w/ thumb.

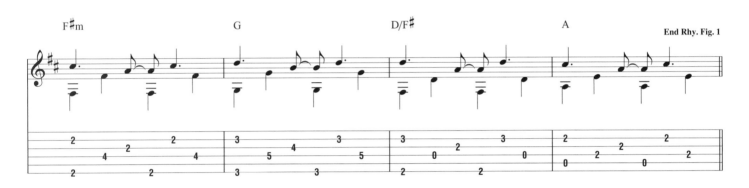

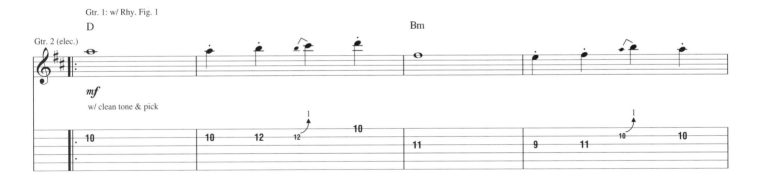

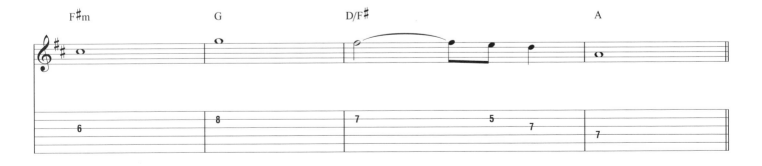

%. Verse

Gtr. 1: w/ Rhy. Fig. 1 (2 times)
Gtr. 2 tacet

1. I hate to see you cry, lying there in
2. You know, it's nothing new. Bad news never
3. *Instrumental…*

that po - si - tion. There's things you need to
had good tim - ing. But then, the cir - cle of your

hear, so turn off your tears and lis - ten.
friends will de - fend the sil - ver lin - ing.

…Instrumental ends

Chorus

Pain throws your heart to the ground.

Gtr. 1

Love turns the whole thing a - round.

Outro

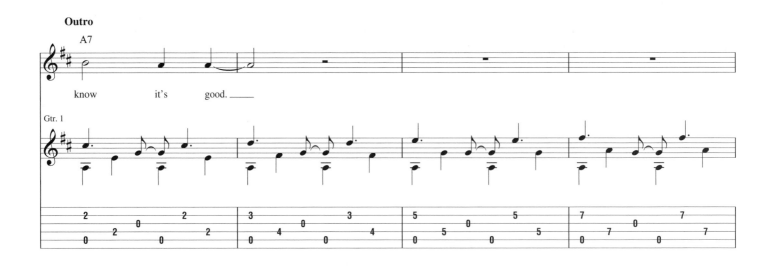

know it's good. ____

Gtr. 1

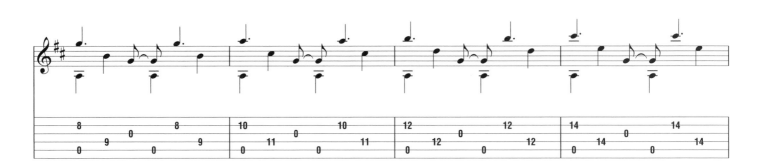

Begin fade

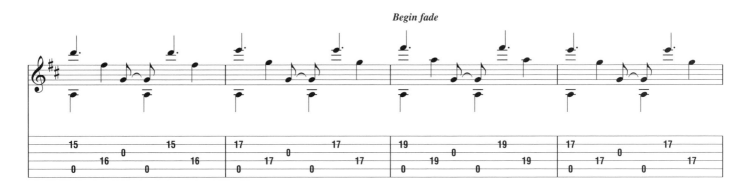

Fade out

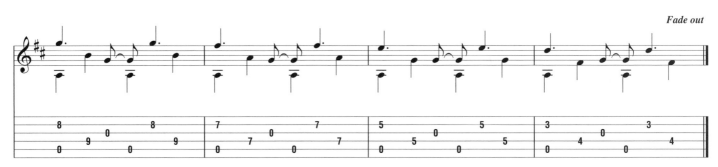

HEARTBREAK WARFARE

Words and Music by
John Mayer

57

LOVE SOON

Words and Music by
John Mayer and Clay Cook

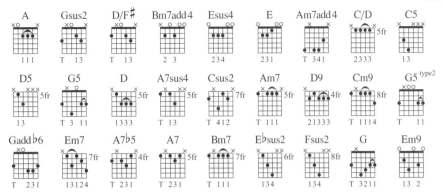

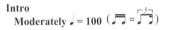

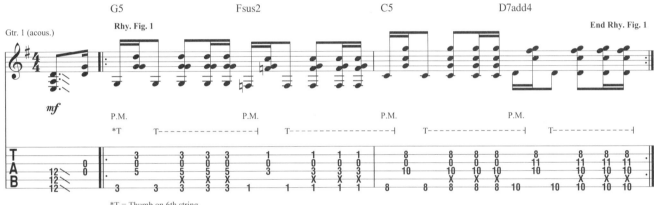

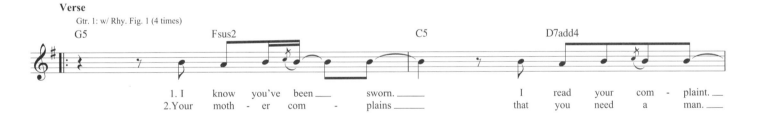

1. I know you've been ___ sworn. ___ I read your com - plaint. ___
2. Your moth - er com - plains ___ that you need a man. ___

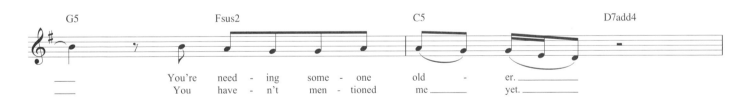

___ You're need - ing some - one old - er. ___
___ You have - n't men - tioned me ___ yet. ___

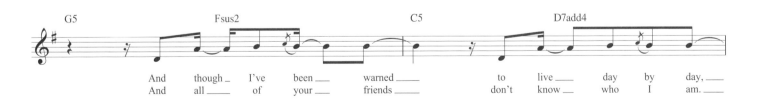

And though ___ I've been ___ warned ___ to live ___ day by day,
And all ___ of your ___ friends ___ don't know ___ who I am.

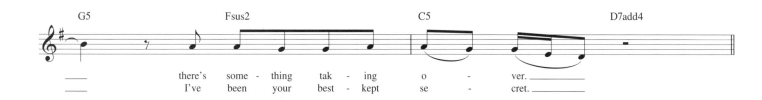

there's some - thing tak - ing o - ver.
I've been your best - kept se - cret.

Pre-Chorus

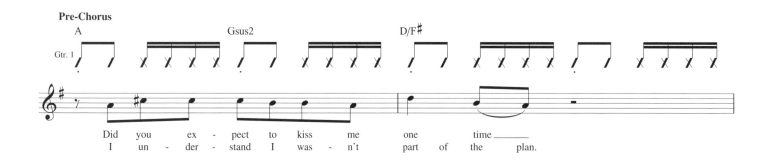

Did you ex - pect to kiss me one time
I un - der - stand I was - n't part of the plan.

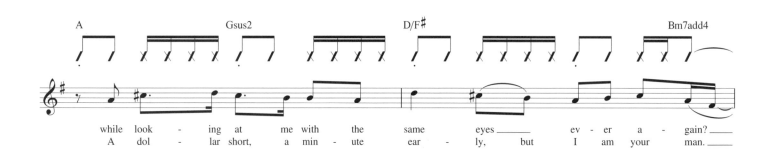

while look - ing at me with the same eyes ev - er a - gain?
A dol - lar short, a min - ute ear - ly, but I am your man.

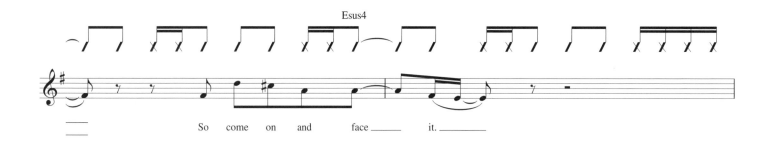

So come on and face it.

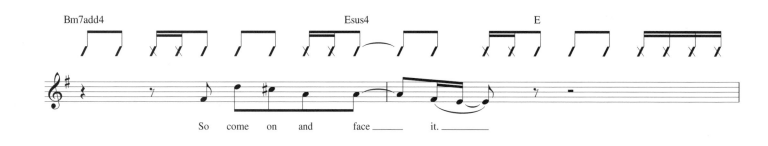

So come on and face it.

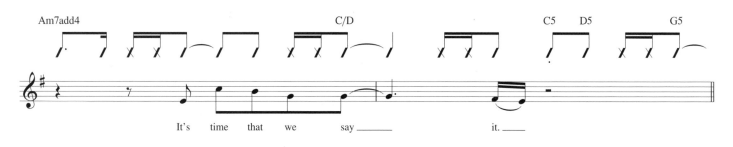

It's time that we say it.

You can cross the line when-ev-er you want to. I'm call-ing it love soon. ___

Close your mind and waste some time if you have to. I'm call-ing it love soon. ___

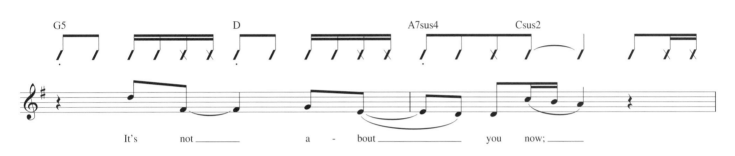

It's not ___ a - bout ___ you now; ___

It's what ___ we are. ___

It's what ___ we are. ___

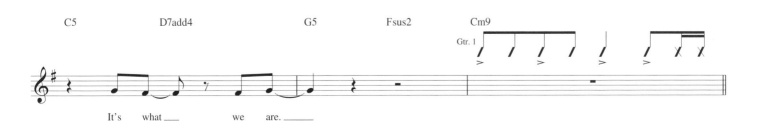

Bridge

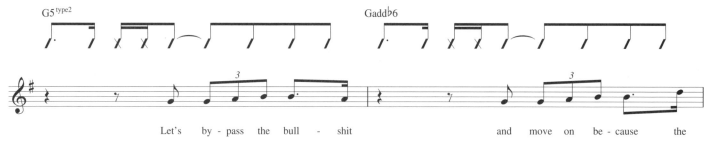

Let's by-pass the bull-shit and move on be-cause the

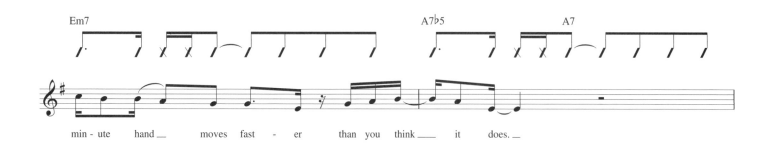

min-ute hand __ moves fast - er than you think __ it does. __

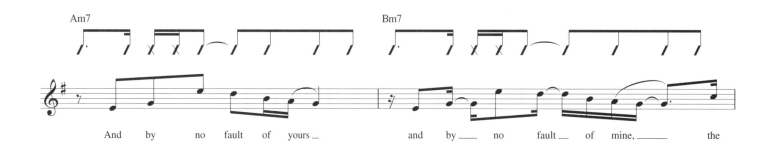

And by no fault of yours __ and by __ no fault __ of mine, ____ the

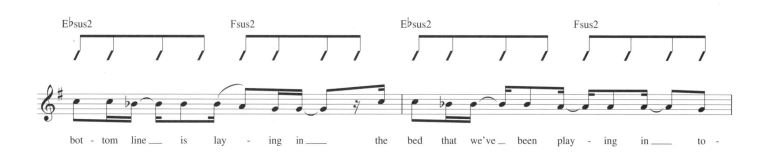

bot - tom line __ is lay - ing in ___ the bed that we've __ been play - ing in ___ to -

Gtr. 1: w/ Rhy. Fig. 1 (2 times)

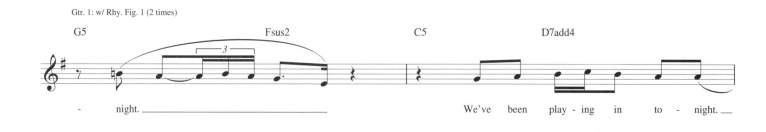

- night. _____ We've been play - ing in to - night. __

Outro-Chorus

I'm call - ing it love soon. __

Gtr. 1: w/ Rhy. Fig. 2 (3 times)

I'm call - ing it love soon. ____

You can cross the line when - ev - er you want to. I'm call - ing it love soon. __

Close your mind and waste some time if you have to. I'm call - ing it love soon. __

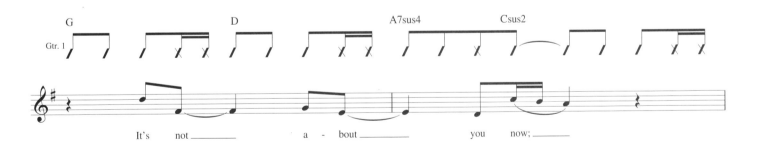

It's not ____ a - bout ____ you now;

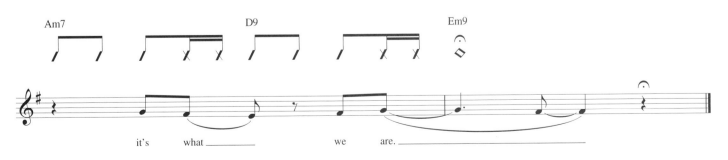

it's what ____ we are. ____

63

MY STUPID MOUTH

Words and Music by
John Mayer

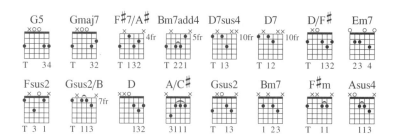

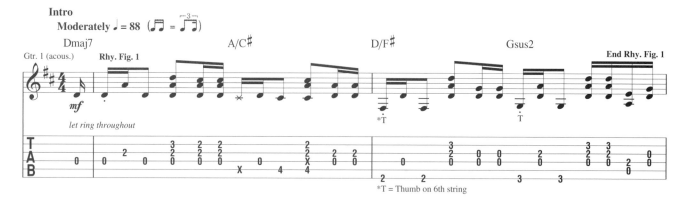

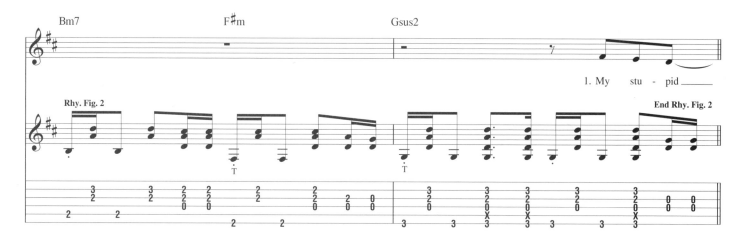

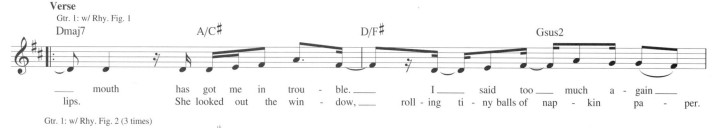

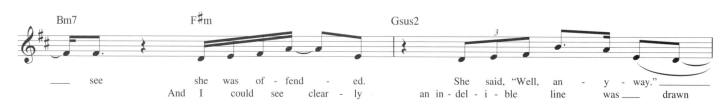

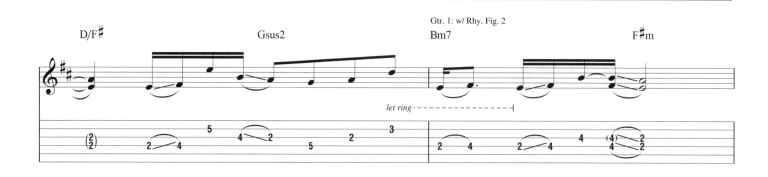

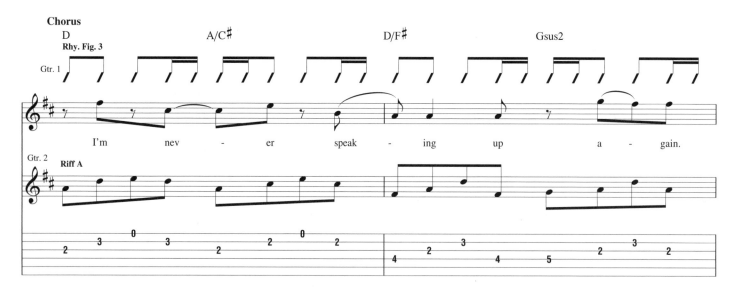

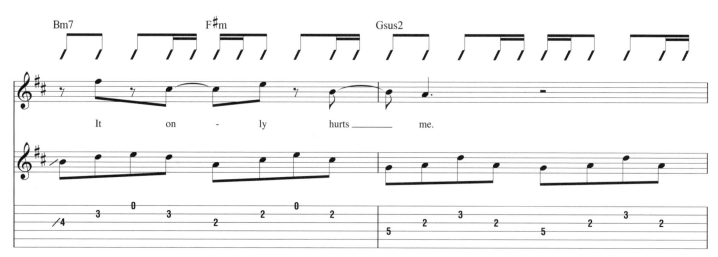

I'd rath - er be _____ a mys - ter - y,

End Rhy. Fig. 3
(cont. in notation)

than she _____ de - sert _____ me.

End Riff A

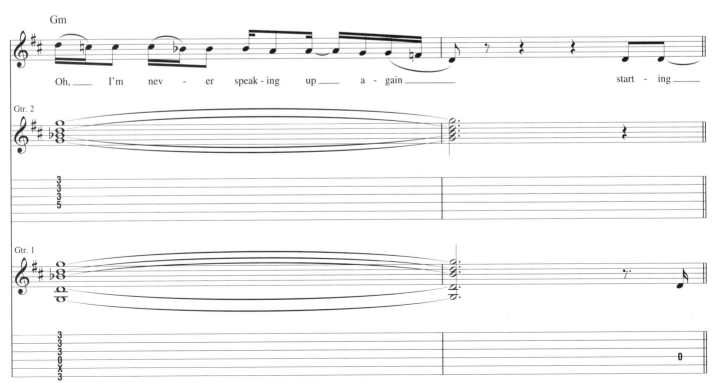

Oh, _____ I'm nev - er speak - ing up _____ a - gain _____ start - ing _____

Gtr. 2

Gtr. 1

Interlude

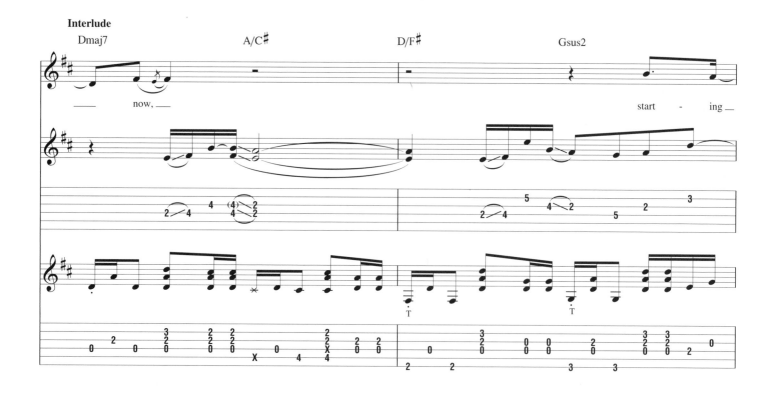

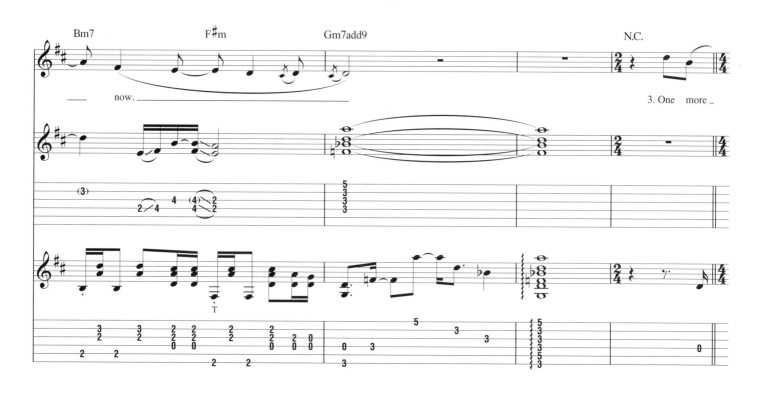

Verse

Gtr. 1: w/ Rhy. Fig. 1
Gtr. 2 tacet

Gtr. 1: w/ Rhy. Fig. 2 (3 times)

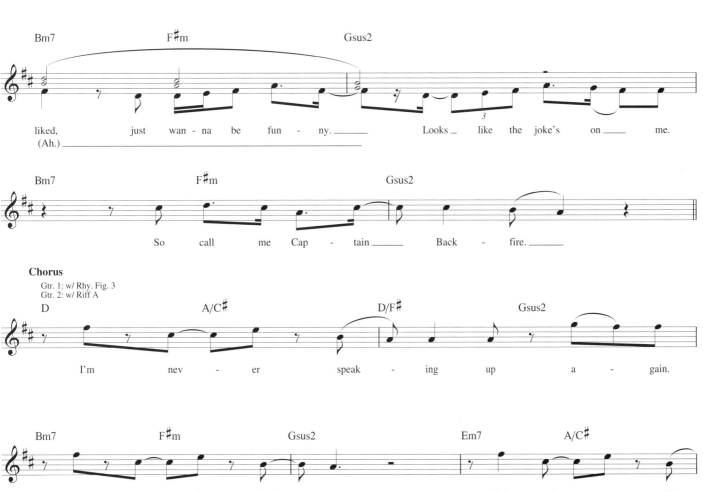

liked, just wan-na be fun-ny._____ Looks__ like the joke's on___ me.
(Ah.)_____

Bm7   F#m   Gsus2

So call me Cap-tain_____ Back - fire._____

Chorus
Gtr. 1: w/ Rhy. Fig. 3
Gtr. 2: w/ Riff A

D   A/C#   D/F#   Gsus2

I'm nev - er speak - ing up a - gain.

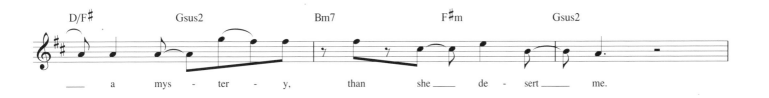

Bm7   F#m   Gsus2   Em7   A/C#

It on - ly hurts___ me. I'd rath - er be___

D/F#   Gsus2   Bm7   F#m   Gsus2

___ a mys - ter - y, than she___ de - sert___ me.

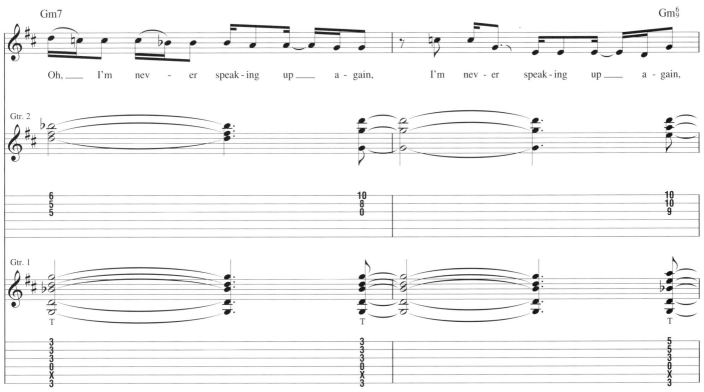

Gm7   Gm⁶₉

Oh,___ I'm nev - er speak-ing up___ a - gain, I'm nev - er speak-ing up___ a - gain,

Gtr. 2

Gtr. 1

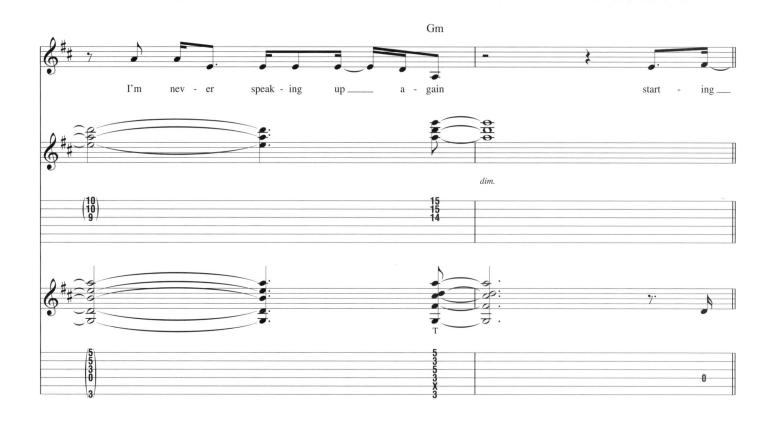

I'm nev-er speak-ing up___ a-gain start-ing___

dim.

Outro

Gtr. 2 tacet

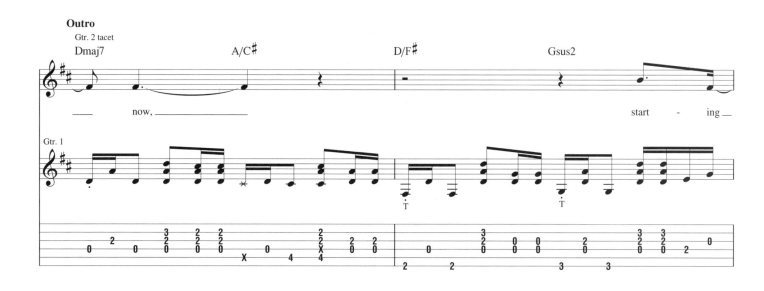

___ now,___ start - ing___

Gtr. 1

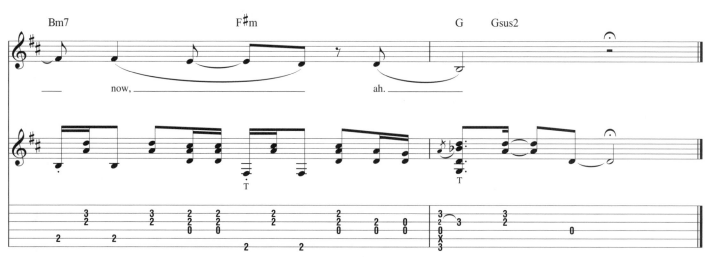

___ now,___ ah.

NEON

Words and Music by
John Mayer and Clay Cook

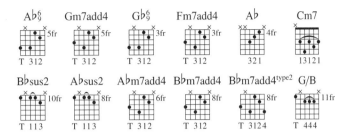

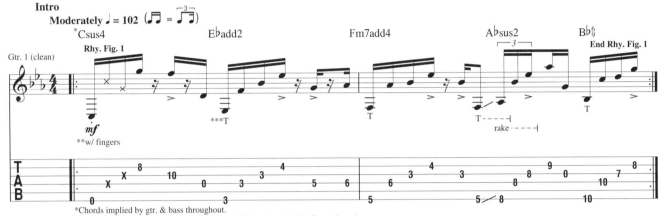

Gtr. 1: Drop C tuning:
(low to high) C-A-D-G-B-E

Intro

Moderately ♩ = 102

Gtr. 1 (clean)

Rhy. Fig. 1

mf
**w/ fingers

*Chords implied by gtr. & bass throughout.
**Fingerpicking pattern: Alternate between R.H. thumb and index finger throughout.
***T = Thumb on 6th string

Verse

Gtr. 1: w/ Rhy. Fig. 1 (4 times)

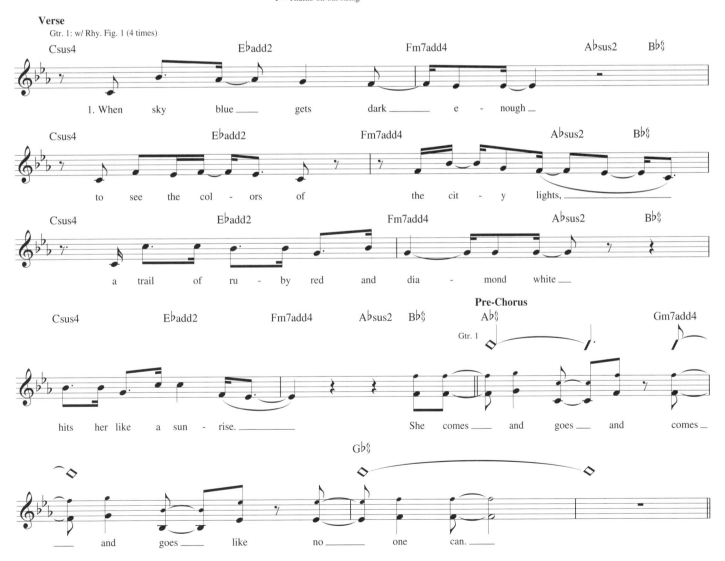

1. When sky blue _____ gets dark e - nough

to see the col - ors of the cit - y lights, _____

a trail of ru - by red and dia - mond white _____

Pre-Chorus

hits her like a sun - rise. _____ She comes _____ and goes _____ and comes _____

_____ and goes _____ like no _____ one can.

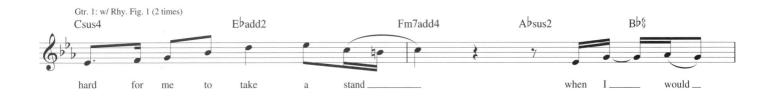

Gtr. 1: w/ Rhy. Fig. 1 (2 times)

Csus4   E♭add2   Fm7add4   A♭sus2   B♭⁶₉

hard   for   me   to   take   a   stand _____ when I _____ would ___

Csus4   E♭add2   Fm7add4   A♭sus2   B♭⁶₉

take   her   an - y   way   I _____ can. _____ She comes ___

Pre-Chorus

Gtr. 1: w/ Rhy. Fig. 3

A♭⁶₉   Gm7add4   G♭⁶₉

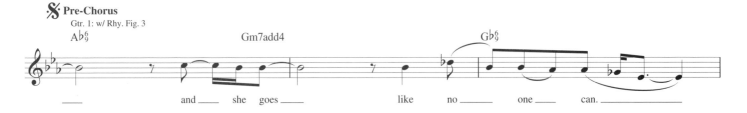

and ___ she goes _____ like   no ___ one ___ can.

A♭⁶₉   Gm7add4

She comes _____ and ___ she goes, _____ she's   slip -

Gtr. 1: w/ Rhy. Fill 1

Fm7add4   Gm7add4   A♭   B♭

- ping   through ___ my   hands. ___ She's al - ways ___ buzz - ing   just   like ___

Chorus

Gtr. 1: w/ Rhy. Fig. 4

Fm7add4   Gm7add4   Cm7   Fm7add4   Gm7add4   Cm7

___ ne - on, _____ ne - on. _____ Ne - on, _____ ne - on.

Fm7add4   Gm7add4   Cm7   B♭

___ Who   knows ___ how   long, _____ how   long, ___ how   long ___

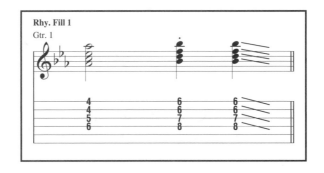

Rhy. Fill 1

Gtr. 1

74

NO SUCH THING

Words by Music by
John Mayer and Clay Cook

*T = Thumb on 6th string

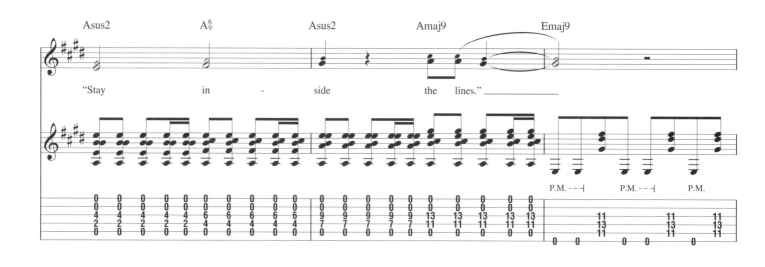

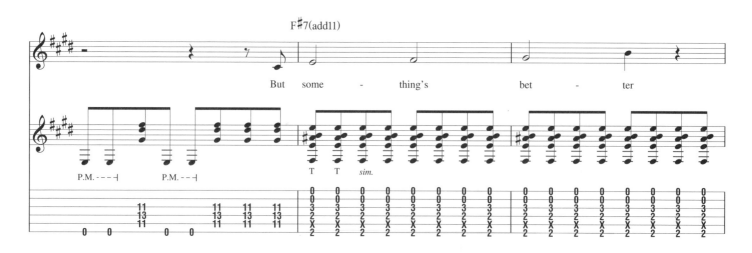

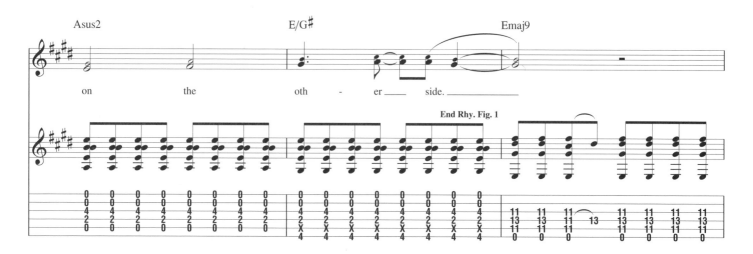

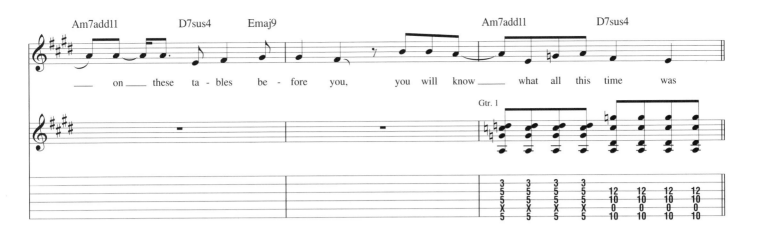

on these ta-bles be-fore you, you will know ____ what all this time was

Outro

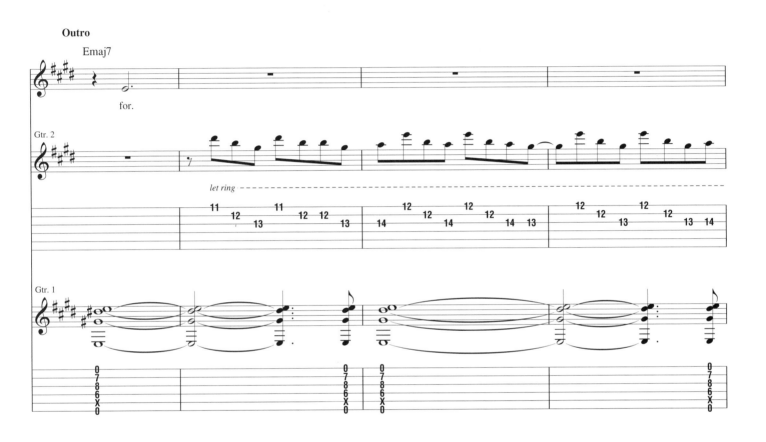

for.

SAY

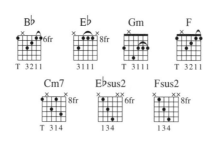

Words and Music by
John Mayer

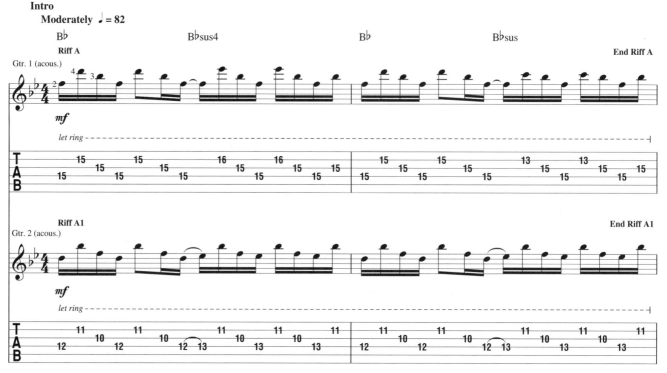

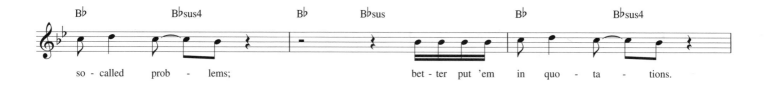

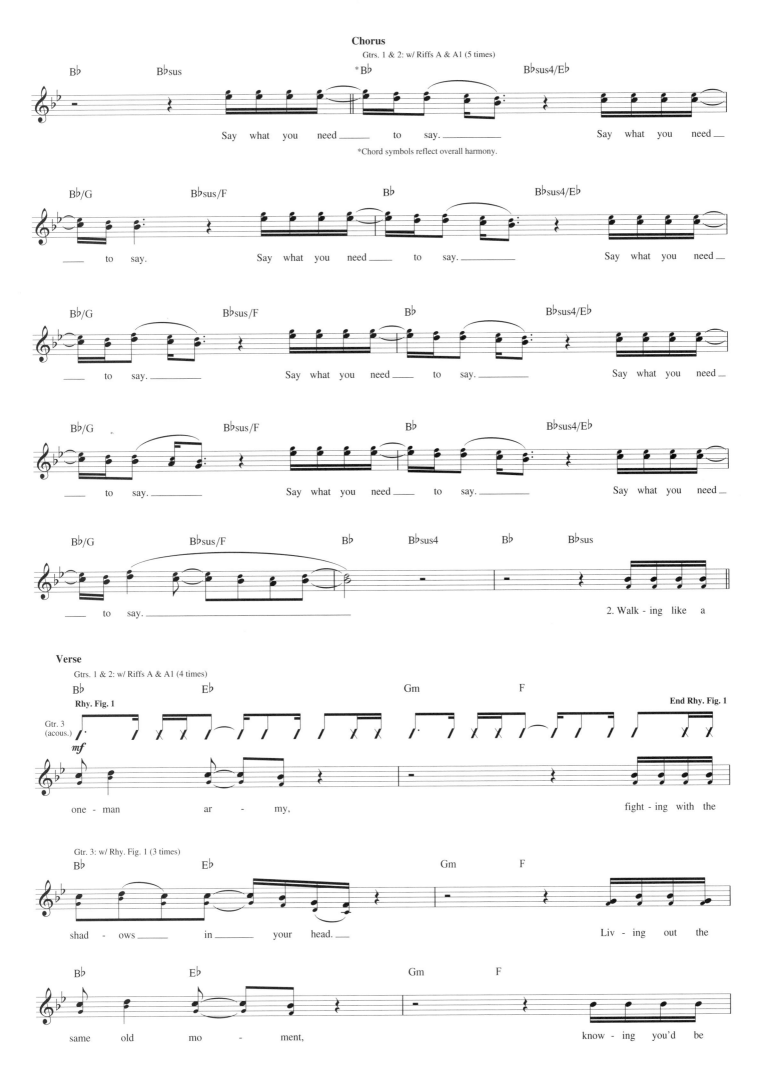

bet - ter ____ off ____ in - stead. _ If you could on - ly _____ say what you need _

Chorus

Gtrs. 1 & 2: w/ Riffs A & A1 (4 times)
Gtr. 3: w/ Rhy. Fig. 1 (4 times)

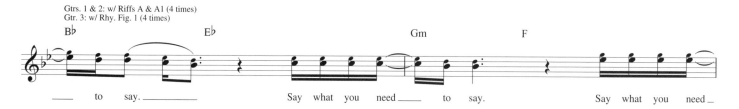

____ to say. _____ Say what you need ____ to say. Say what you need _

____ to say. _____ Say what you need ____ to say. _____ Say what you need _

____ to say. _____ Say what you need ____ to say. _____ Say what you need _

____ to say. _____ Say what you need ____ to say. _____

Bridge

Gtrs. 1 & 2: w/ Riffs A & A1 (3 times)

____ Have no fear _____ for giv - ing in. _____

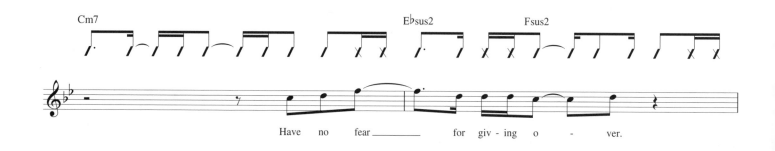

Have no fear _____ for giv - ing o - ver.

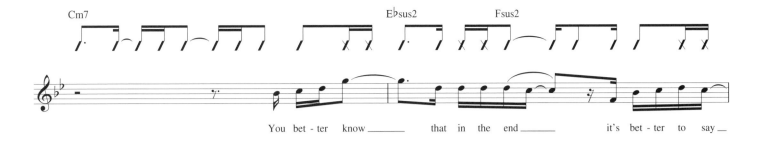

You bet - ter know _____ that in the end _____ it's bet - ter to say _____

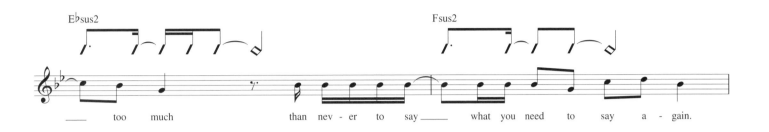

_____ too much than nev - er to say _____ what you need to say a - gain.

Verse

Gtrs. 1 & 2: w/ Riffs A & A1
Gtr. 3 tacet
Gtrs. 1 & 2: w/ Riffs A & A1 (4 times)

3. E - ven if your hands are shak - ing and your

faith is bro - ken; e - ven as the eyes are clos - ing,

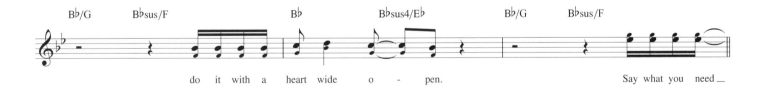

do it with a heart wide o - pen. Say what you need _____

Chorus

Gtrs. 1 & 2: w/ Riffs A & A1 (4 times)

Rhy. Fig. 2

End Rhy. Fig. 2

Gtr. 3

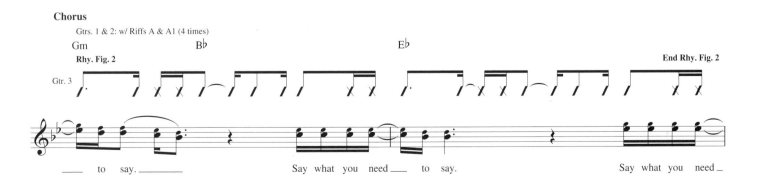

_____ to say. _____ Say what you need _____ to say. Say what you need _____

Gtr. 3: w/ Rhy. Fig. 2 (3 times)

Gm   B♭   E♭

_____ to say.   Say what you need ____ to say. _____   Say what you need ____

Gm   B♭   E♭

_____ to say.   Say what you need ____ to say. _____   Say what you need ____

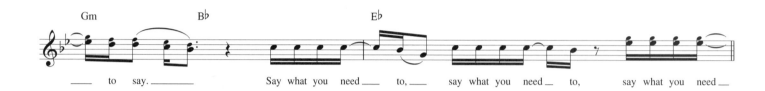

Gm   B♭   E♭

_____ to say. _____   Say what you need ____ to, ____ say what you need ___ to,   say what you need ____

Outro-Chorus

Gtrs. 1 & 2: w/ Riffs A & A1 (till end)
Gtr. 3: w/ Rhy. Fig. 2 (till end)

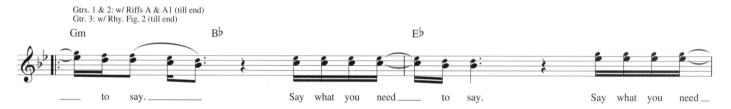

Gm   B♭   E♭

_____ to say. _____   Say what you need ____ to say.   Say what you need ____

Gm   B♭   E♭

_____ to say. _____   Say what you need ____ to say. _____   Say what you need ____

Gm   B♭   E♭

_____ to say. _____   Say what you need ____ to say. _____   Say what you need ____

Repeat and fade

Gm   B♭   E♭

_____ to say. _____   Say what you need ____ to say. _____   Say what you need ___

SLOW DANCING IN A BURNING ROOM

Words and Music by
John Mayer

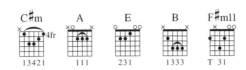

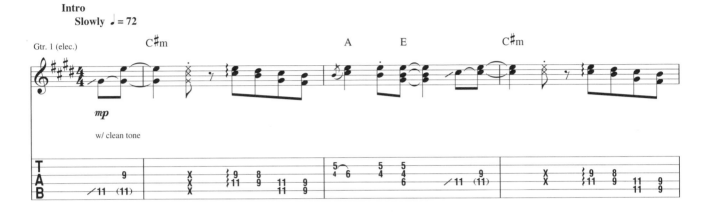

*Strum w/ all downstrokes (throughout).

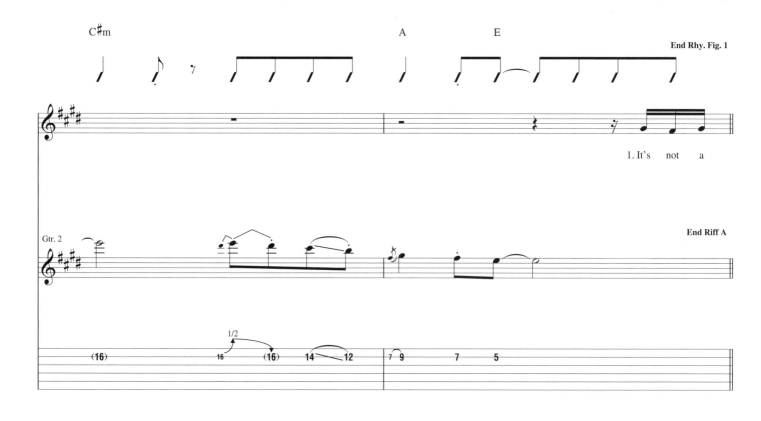

Verse

sil - ly lit - tle mo - ment,   it's not the storm be - fore __ the calm. _____   This is the
one you al - ways dreamed of,   you were the one I tried __ to draw. _____   How dare you

deep and dy - ing breath of   this love that we've been work - ing on. _____   Can't seem to
say it's noth - ing to me.   Ba - by, you're the on - ly light __ I ev - er saw. _____   I'll make the

hold you like I want to,   so I can feel you in ___ my arms. _____   No - bod - y's
most of all the sad - ness,   you'll be a bitch be - cause __ you can. _____   You try to

gon - na come and save   you,   we pulled too man - y false __ a - larms.   We're go - ing
hit me just to hurt me so you leave me feel - ing dirt - y 'cause you can't un - der - stand.

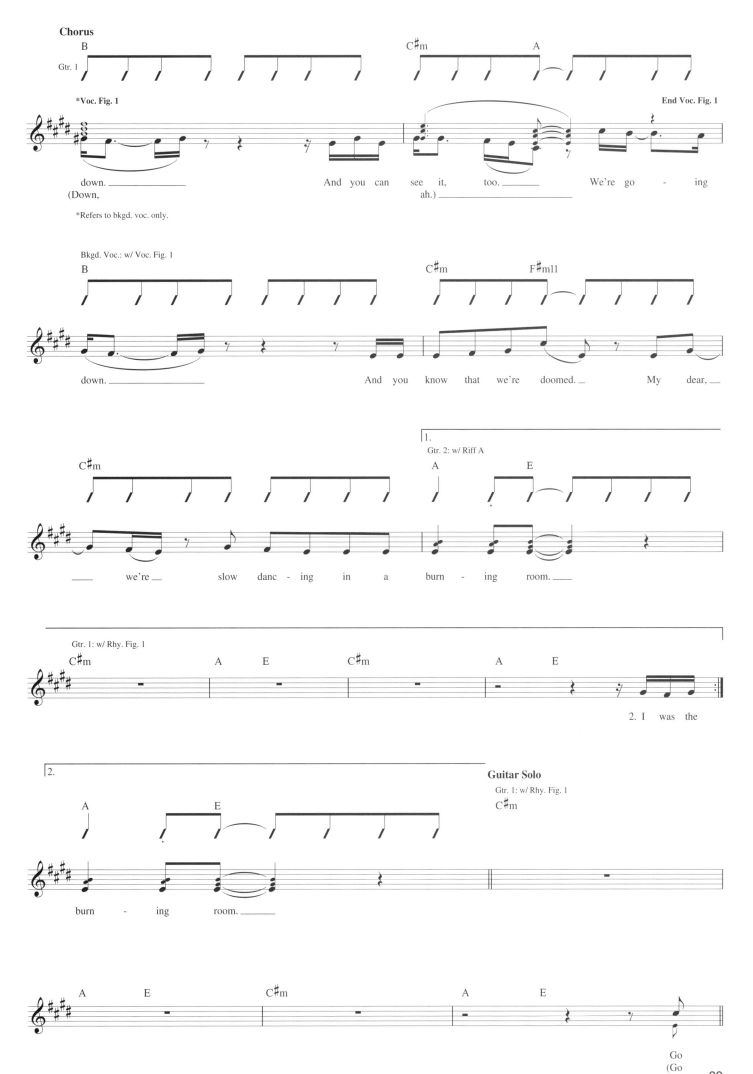

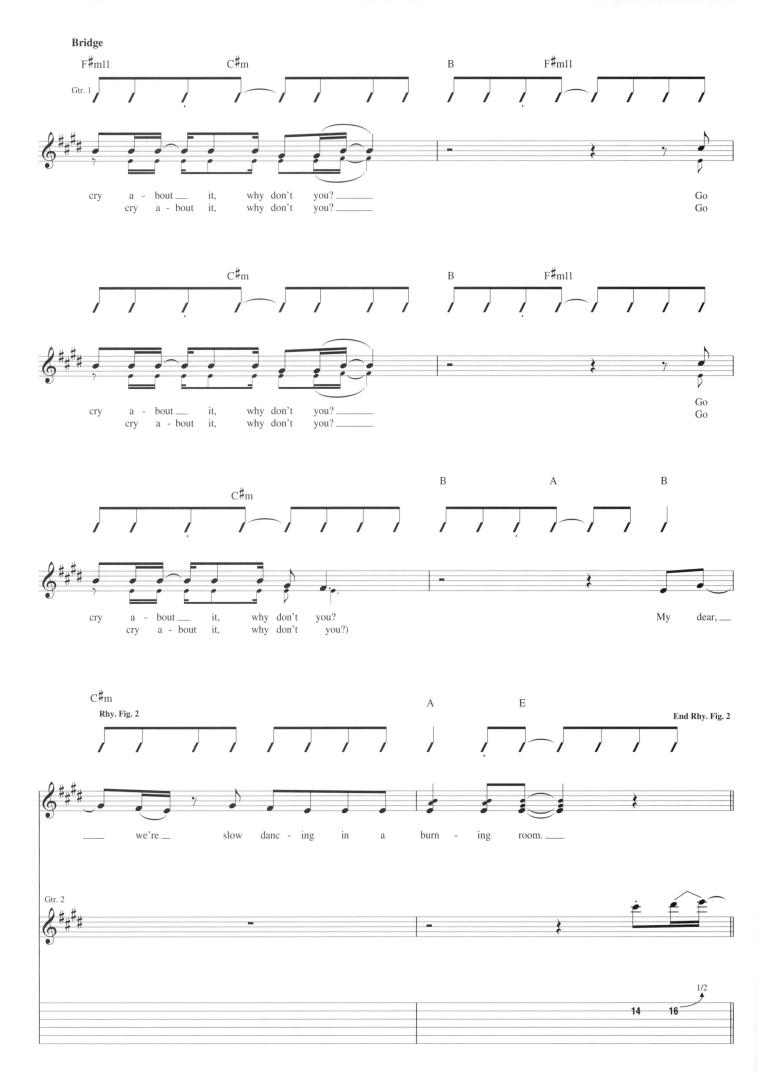

Outro

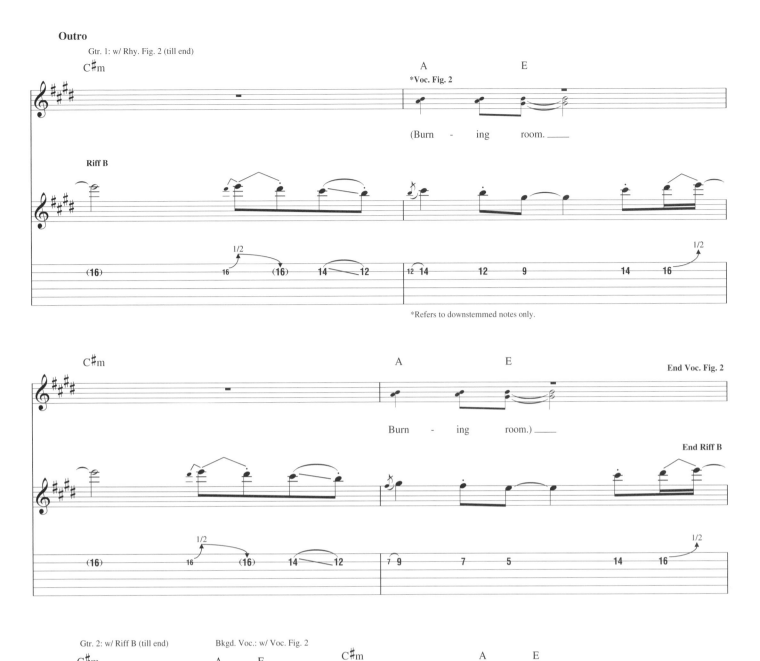

*Refers to downstemmed notes only.

VICTORIA

Words and Music by
John Mayer

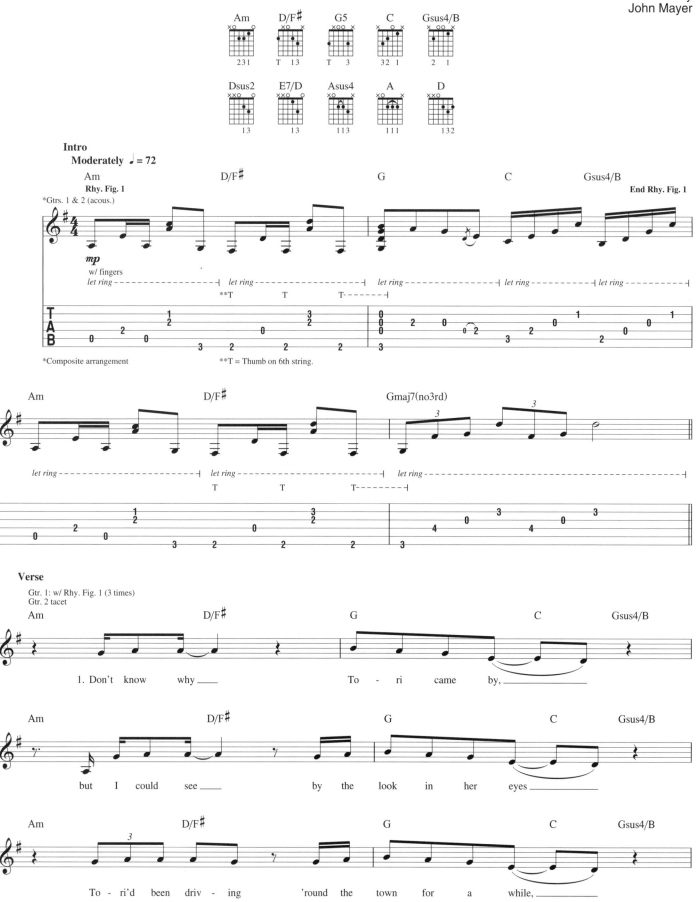

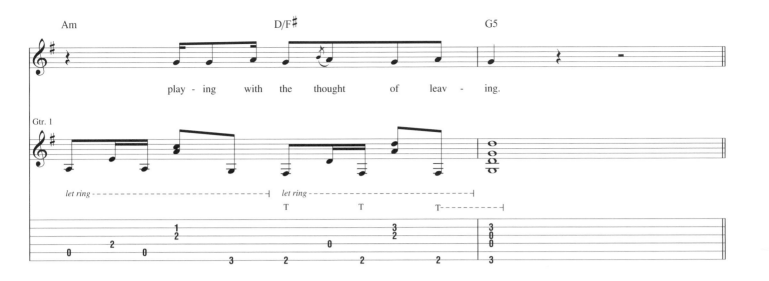

Verse

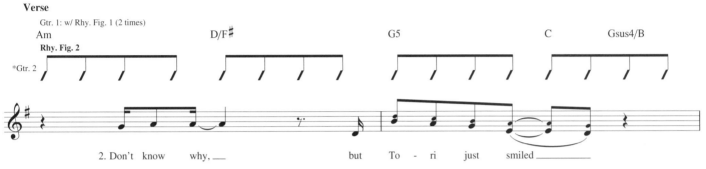

*w/ pick; strum w/ all downstrokers

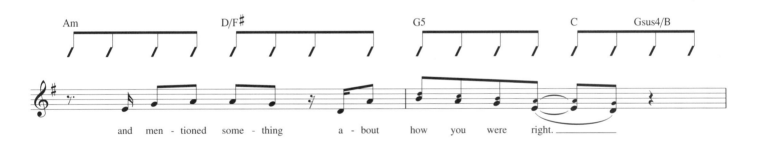

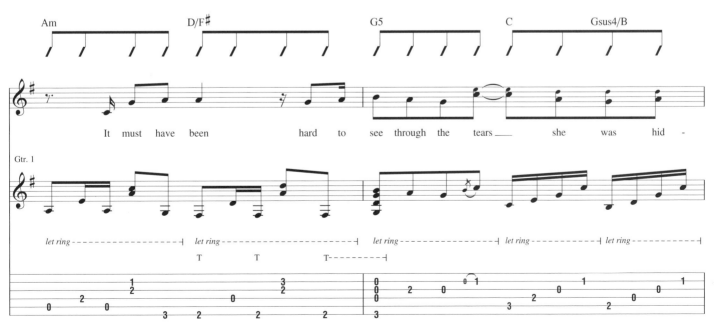

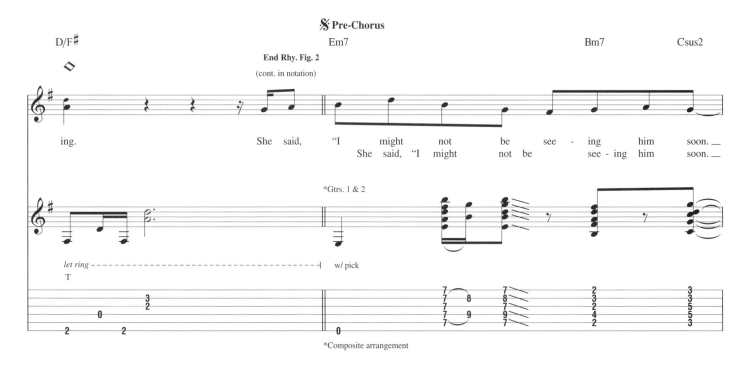

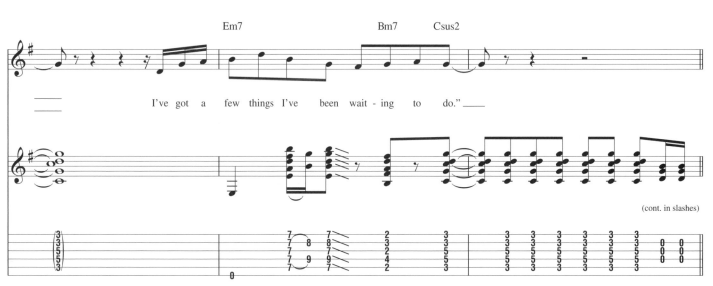

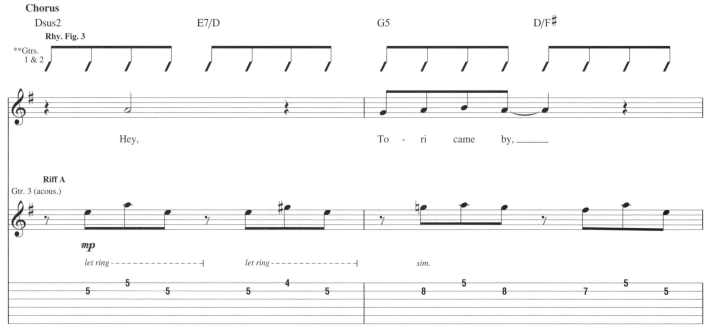

**Strum w/ all downstrokes.

94

Verse

and the suit-case on the back seat in-side;

D.S. al Coda

sure, it's so ___ she can't look out be-hind ___ at the road. _

⊕ Coda

Interlude

Gtrs. 1 & 2: w/ Rhy. Fig. 2

Gtr. 4 (acous.)

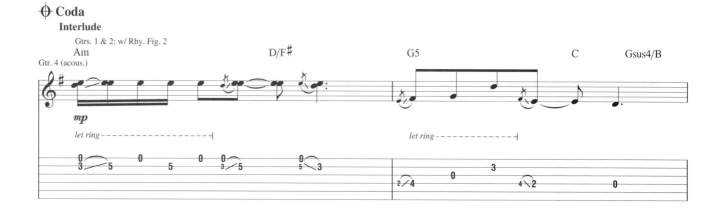

let ring

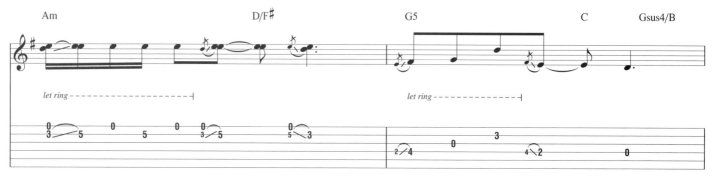

let ring

96

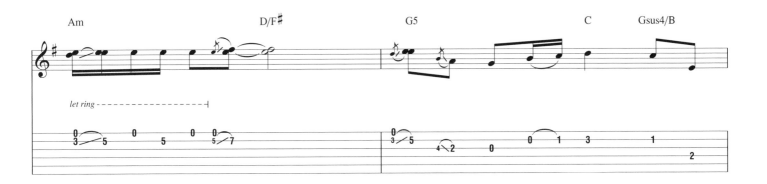

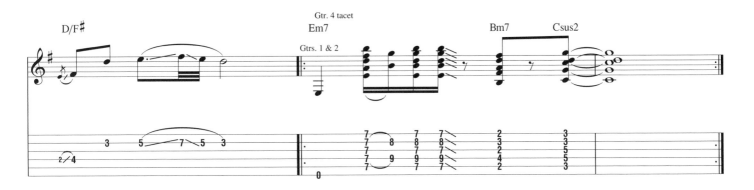

Verse

Gtr. 1: w/ Rhy. Fig. 1 (2 times)
Gtr. 2 tacet

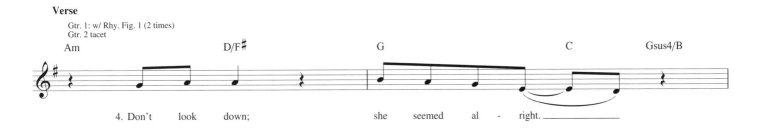

4. Don't look down; she seemed al - right. _____

You might be ask - ing, "Where is To - ri to - night?" _____

Some - where out on the high - way; I'm sure ___ that she's fine. _____

VULTURES

Words and Music by
John Mayer, Pino Paladino
and Steven Jordan

Verse

Gtr. 1: w/ Riff A (2 times)

F#m11

3. Wheels up, I got to leave this eve - ning. I can't seem to shake these vul - tures

off of my trail. Pow - er is made by pow - er be - ing tak - en.

D.S. al Coda 2

So I keep on run - ning to pro - tect my sit - u - a - tion.

Coda 2

Gtr. 1: w/ Riff B

Interlude

Gtr. 1: w/ Riff A (2 times)

Amaj9

test - ing me, test - ing me. Whoo,

B⁶/₉sus4   Amaj9

whoo. Whoo,

B⁶/₉sus4

whoo.

Outro

Gtr. 1: w/ Riff A (2 times)

F#m11

What you gon - na do a - bout it? What you gon - na do a - bout it?

What you gon - na do a - bout it?

Gtr. 1: w/ Riff A (till end)

F#m11

Don't give up, give up. Don't

Repeat and fade

give up, give up, give up. Don't

WAITING ON THE WORLD TO CHANGE

Words and Music by
John Mayer

WHO SAYS

Words and Music by
John Mayer

%️ **Verse**

Gtr. 1: w/ Rhy. Fig. 1

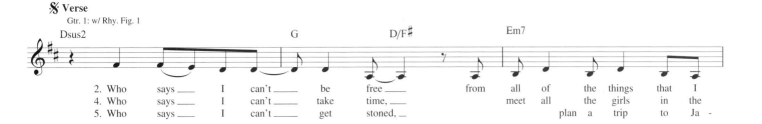

2. Who says ____ I can't ____ be free ____ from all of the things that I
4. Who says ____ I can't ____ take time, ____ meet all the girls in the
5. Who says ____ I can't ____ get stoned, ____ plan a trip to Ja -

used to be? ____ Re - write ____ my his - to - ry. Who ____
coun - ty line? ____ Wait on fate to send a sign. Who ____
pan a - lone? ____ Does - n't mat - ter if I e - ven go. Who ____

____ says I can't be free?
____ says I can't take time?
____ says I can't get stoned?

It's been a long ____

Chorus

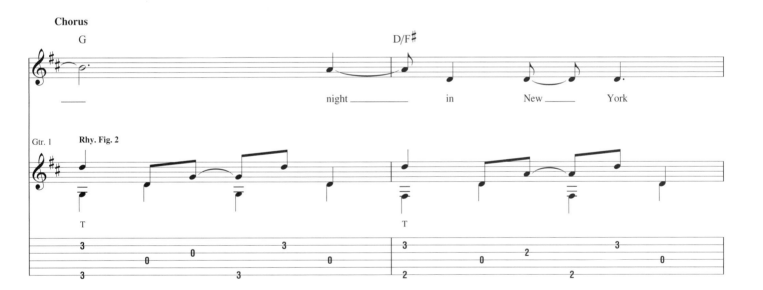

night ____ in New ____ York

Gtr. 1   **Rhy. Fig. 2**

T   T

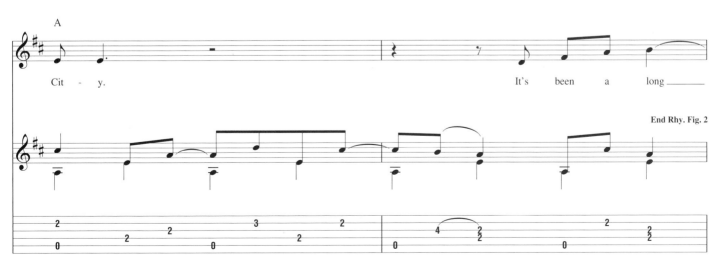

Cit - y.   It's been a long ____

End Rhy. Fig. 2

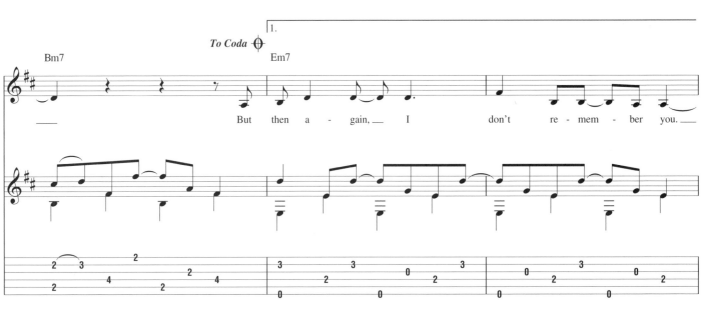
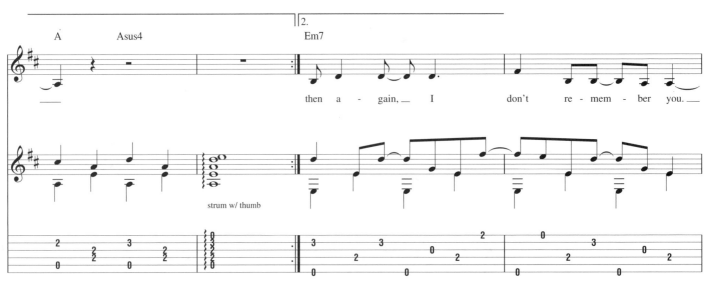

Coda

then a - gain, __ I don't re - mem - ber, don't re - mem - ber you. __

Outro

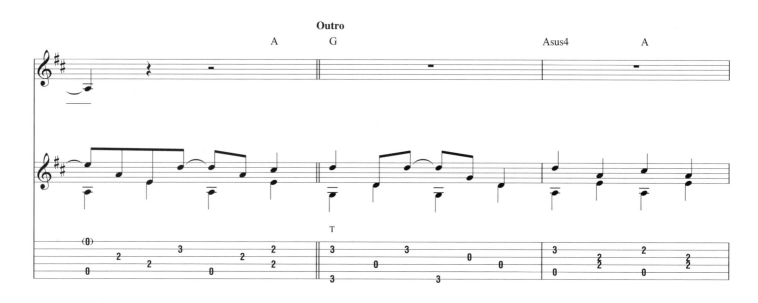

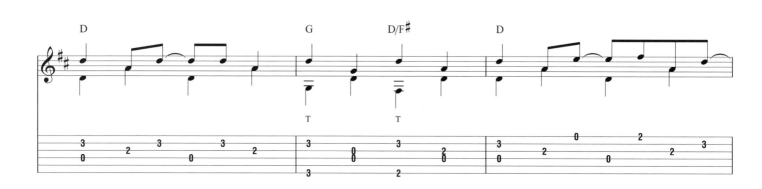

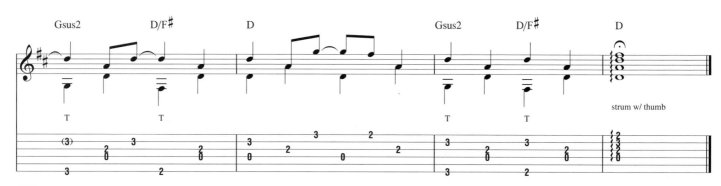

WHY GEORGIA

Words and Music by
John Mayer

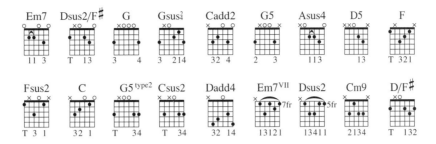

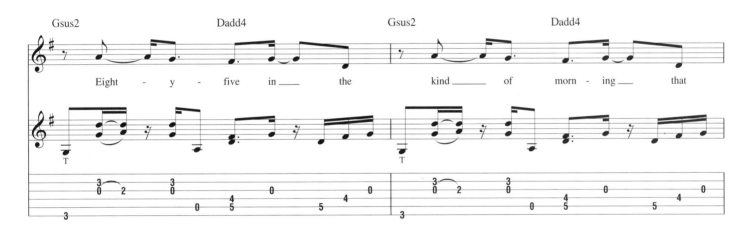

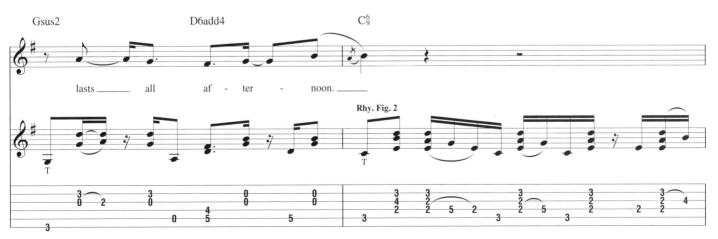

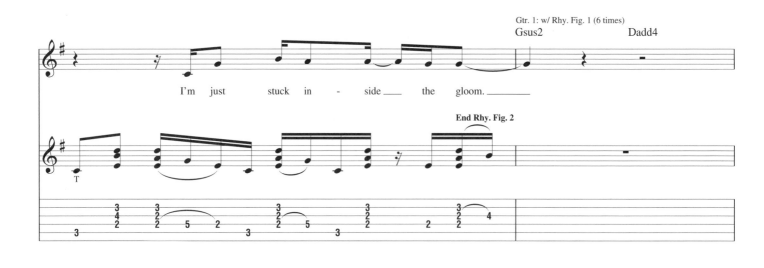

I'm just stuck in - side____ the gloom._____

Four____ more ex - its____ to my____ a - part - ment,_ but

I____ am tempt - ed____ to keep____ the car in____ drive,____

and leave_ it all be - hind.____ 'Cause I____

Pre-Chorus

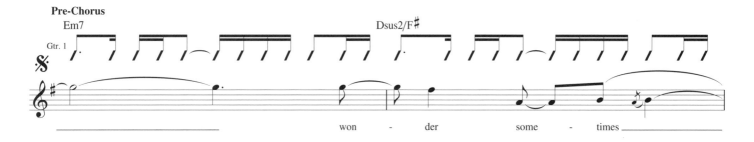

_____ won - der some - times_____

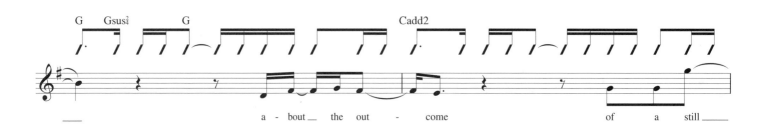

____ a - bout__ the out - come of a still____

_____ ver - dict - less___ life._____ Am I

110

YOUR BODY IS A WONDERLAND

Words and Music by
John Mayer

Drop D tuning:
(low to high) D-A-D-G-B-E

Intro

Moderate Rock ♩ = 94

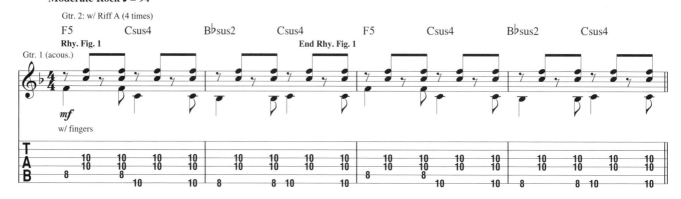

Verse

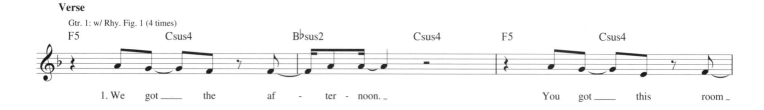

1. We got ___ the af - ter - noon. ___   You got ___ this room ___

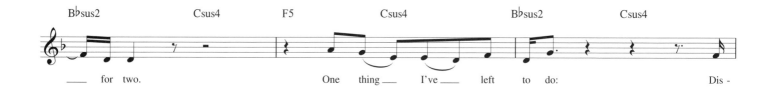

___ for two.   One thing ___ I've ___ left to do: Dis -

Verse
Gtr. 1: w/ Rhy. Fig. 1 (4 times)
Gtr. 2: w/ Riff A (8 times)

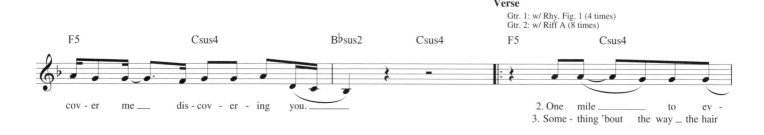

cov - er me ___ dis - cov - er - ing you. ___   2. One mile ___ to ev -
                                                             3. Some - thing 'bout the way ___ the hair

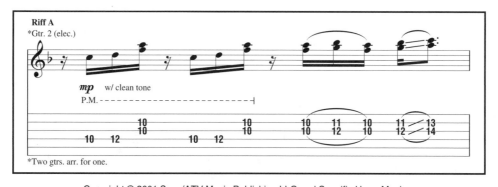

*Two gtrs. arr. for one.

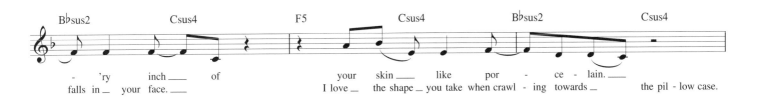

-'ry inch ___ of / falls in ___ your face. ___   your skin ___ like por - ce - lain. ___   I love ___ the shape ___ you take when crawl - ing towards ___   the pil - low case.

One pair ___ of can - dy lips ___ and / You tell ___ me where ___ to go, ___ and   though I might leave ___ to find ___ it, I'll   your bub - ble - gum tongue. / nev - er let ___ your head ___ hit the bed

Pre-Chorus
Gtr. 2: w/ Riff A (8 times)

And if you want ___ love, ___ / with - out ___ my hand ___ be - hind ___ it. You want love?   we'll make ___ it } / We'll make ___ it }   swim - ming a deep ___

Rhy. Fig. 2
Gtr. 1
End Rhy. Fig. 2

*T ------- | T ----------- |

*T = Thumb on 6th string

Gtr. 1: w/ Rhy. Fig. 2 (2 times)

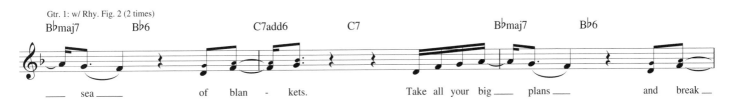

___ sea ___ of blan - kets.   Take all your big ___ plans ___   and break ___

___ 'em.   This is bound ___ to be a - while.   Your bod - y is a won -
(Ah.) ___

Gtr. 1

T   T   *sim.*

Chorus
Gtr. 1: w/ Rhy. Fig. 1 (3 times)

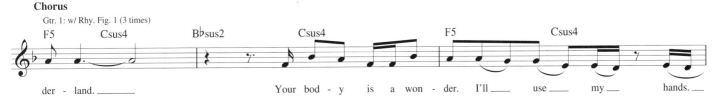

der - land. ___   Your bod - y is a won - der. I'll ___ use ___ my ___ hands. ___

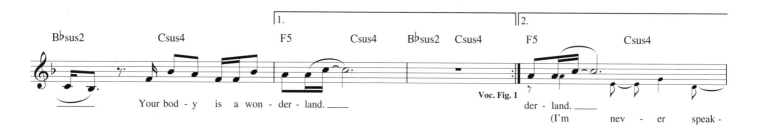

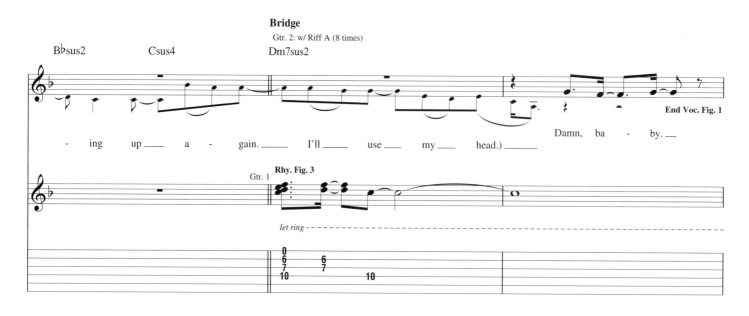

Guitar Solo

Gtr. 1: w/ Rhy. Fig. 3 (2 times)
Gtr. 2: w/ Riff A (8 times)

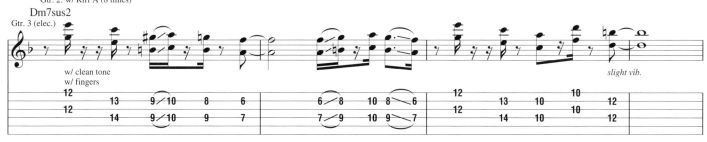

Interlude

Chorus
Gtr. 1: w/ Rhy. Fig. 1 (4 times)
Gtr. 2: w/ Riff A (8 times)
Bkgd. Voc.: w/ Voc. Fig. 1 (2 times)

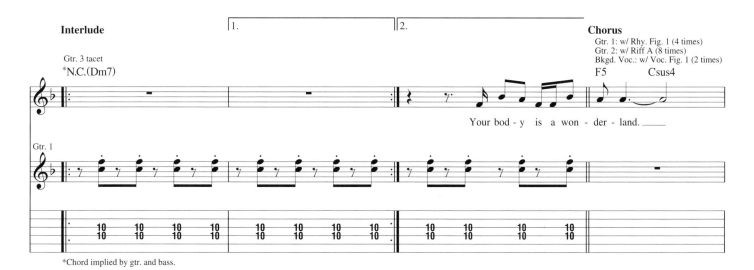

*Chord implied by gtr. and bass.

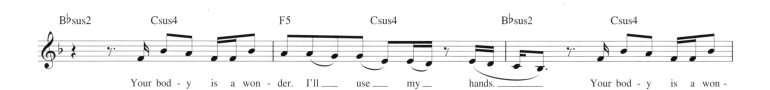

Your bod - y is a won - der. I'll ___ use ___ my ___ hands. ___ Your bod - y is a won -

der - land. ___ Your bod - y is ___ a won - der - land. ___

Outro

Gtr. 1: w/ Rhy. Fig. 1
Gtr. 2: w/ Riff A (2 times)

Repeat and fade

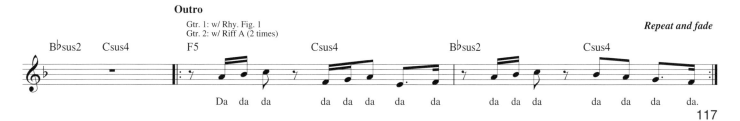

Da da da   da da da da da   da da da   da da da da.

117

GUITAR NOTATION LEGEND

Guitar music can be notated three different ways: on a *musical staff*, in *tablature*, and in *rhythm slashes*.

RHYTHM SLASHES are written above the staff. Strum chords in the rhythm indicated. Use the chord diagrams found at the top of the first page of the transcription for the appropriate chord voicings. Round noteheads indicate single notes.

THE MUSICAL STAFF shows pitches and rhythms and is divided by bar lines into measures. Pitches are named after the first seven letters of the alphabet.

TABLATURE graphically represents the guitar fingerboard. Each horizontal line represents a string, and each number represents a fret.

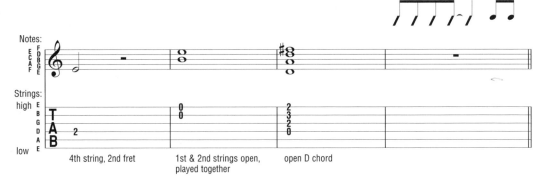

4th string, 2nd fret   1st & 2nd strings open, played together   open D chord

HALF-STEP BEND: Strike the note and bend up 1/2 step.

WHOLE-STEP BEND: Strike the note and bend up one step.

GRACE NOTE BEND: Strike the note and immediately bend up as indicated.

SLIGHT (MICROTONE) BEND: Strike the note and bend up 1/4 step.

BEND AND RELEASE: Strike the note and bend up as indicated, then release back to the original note. Only the first note is struck.

PRE-BEND: Bend the note as indicated, then strike it.

VIBRATO: The string is vibrated by rapidly bending and releasing the note with the fretting hand.

WIDE VIBRATO: The pitch is varied to a greater degree by vibrating with the fretting hand.

HAMMER-ON: Strike the first (lower) note with one finger, then sound the higher note (on the same string) with another finger by fretting it without picking.

PULL-OFF: Place both fingers on the notes to be sounded. Strike the first note and without picking, pull the finger off to sound the second (lower) note.

LEGATO SLIDE: Strike the first note and then slide the same fret-hand finger up or down to the second note. The second note is not struck.

SHIFT SLIDE: Same as legato slide, except the second note is struck.

TRILL: Very rapidly alternate between the notes indicated by continuously hammering on and pulling off.

TAPPING: Hammer ("tap") the fret indicated with the pick-hand index or middle finger and pull off to the note fretted by the fret hand.

NATURAL HARMONIC: Strike the note while the fret-hand lightly touches the string directly over the fret indicated.

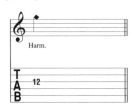

PINCH HARMONIC: The note is fretted normally and a harmonic is produced by adding the edge of the thumb or the tip of the index finger of the pick hand to the normal pick attack.

PICK SCRAPE: The edge of the pick is rubbed down (or up) the string, producing a scratchy sound.

MUFFLED STRINGS: A percussive sound is produced by laying the fret hand across the string(s) without depressing, and striking them with the pick hand.

PALM MUTING: The note is partially muted by the pick hand lightly touching the string(s) just before the bridge.

RAKE: Drag the pick across the strings indicated with a single motion.

TREMOLO PICKING: The note is picked as rapidly and continuously as possible.

VIBRATO BAR DIVE AND RETURN: The pitch of the note or chord is dropped a specified number of steps (in rhythm), then returned to the original pitch.

VIBRATO BAR SCOOP: Depress the bar just before striking the note, then quickly release the bar.

VIBRATO BAR DIP: Strike the note and then immediately drop a specified number of steps, then release back to the original pitch.